Cooperative Learning and Achievement

ABOUT THE AUTHOR

PANNEER SELVAM is born in Salem - Valappady of Tamil Nadu. He started his career as school teacher in New Delhi in the year 1991. He joins as lecturer in DIET, perundurai of Erode in 2000. Bharathiyar University were gave the Philosophy in Doctorates in Language and Education. He is the seventh diploma holder from National University of Educational Planning and Administration (NUEPA), New Delhi in 2002. In 2005, the Tamil Nadu government was given the 'Excellence Award' for his unrivalled teaching activities and some organization also. He has published more than hundreds of Research Papers and books in the field of Education. At present he is working in the department of Education, Bharathidasan University, Tamil Nadu.

ABOUT THE BOOK

Education by its emphases practices the slaying of Sir William Hamilton, "In the world there is nothing great but man; in man there is nothing great but mind". Education shows us a development, the unrealized powers of mind through exercise becoming actualized. Education is the process of evolution which becomes conscious of itself. As a significant conscious process of development in time, whereby immaturity reaches maturity and the child becomes a man, education ought to be a chapter in the serial which universe is writing through time in the heavens and upon the earth. Cooperative Learning is a very formal way of structuring activities in a learning environment that includes specific elements intended to increase the potential for rich and deep learning by the students.

❐

Cooperative Learning and Achievement

Dr. S.K. Panneer Selvam
Assistant Professor, Department of Education
Bharathidasan University, T.N.,India

AMIGA PRESS INC.

AMIGA PRESS INC.
H.O:- 28-A, Indra Park, St.No-9
Near-Chander Nagar, Krishna Nagar
Delhi: - 110051 (India)
Tel: - 011-22504028, +91-98736-57000
Email: - amigapress@gmail.com
info@amigapress.co.in
amigaeditorial@gmail.com
amigapub@gmail.com

Website: - www.amigapress.co.in

This edition is published by Amiga Press Inc.

ISBN: 978-93-84533-66-3

First Published 2020

Printed and bound in India by Replika Press Pvt. Ltd.

Contents

❐

1

Problem and its Perspectives

Shame and guilt are two closely related self-conscious emotions of negative affect that give rise to disparate motivational and self-regulatory behaviors (Tangney & Dearing, 2002). While shame has been associated with a host of maladaptive functioning variables and life difficulties, guilt has been consistently associated with adaptive self-regulation outcomes (Tangney, Stuewig, & Mashek, 2007). In recent times, several researchers have begun to explore the respective implications of shame and guilt-proneness for the experience of substance use-related disorders (e.g. Dearing, Stuewig, & Tangney, 2005; Meehan et al., 1996; O'Conner, Berry, Inaba, Weiss, & Morrison, 1994). Preliminary research suggests that while guilt-proneness is inversely related to alcohol misuse, shame-proneness appears to share a positive relationship with alcohol problems (Dearing et al., 2005).

In elaborating upon the apparent link between shame and alcohol problems, several theorists have hypothesized that shame-prone individuals may be inclined to drink as a means of down-regulating experiences of shame and other negative affect (Dearing et al., 2005; Potter-Efron, 2002; Stuewig & Tangney, 2007; Tangney & Dearing, 2002; Wiechelt, 2007). While this drinking-to-cope strategy may be effective in the short term, Tangney and Dearing (2002) suggest that a destructive cycle of negative effect, alcohol use, and the experience of negative alcohol use-related consequences may result if 2 this substance use as a coping strategy is frequently relied upon. Providing additional support for the existence of a —shame-alcohol use shame spiral‖, experiences of shame are commonly experienced as a result of alcohol problems and it appears that shame, in particular, serves as a substantial barrier to treatment seeking behavior and positive therapeutic outcomes (Potter-Efron, 2002).

The preliminary and relatively scant empirical literature on shame, guilt, and alcohol use has thus far sought to examine the relationships between generalized shame and guilt-proneness and the experience of alcohol problems (see Dearing et al., 2005). However, it appears no research has sought to directly explore the reasons for which shame and guilt-prone individuals consume alcohol. Similarly, it does not appear that any research has been conducted to determine whether or not shame-prone individuals are actually inclined to drink to down-regulate negative effect.

Moreover, relatively little attention has been paid to the correlates of shame and guilt experienced specifically as a result of alcohol problems and negative alcohol-related consequences. A likely reason for this dearth in the literature is that while there are valid and reliable measures that assess dispositional shame and guilt-proneness (see Tangney & Dearing, 2002), there is currently no measure that quantitatively assesses shame and guilt reactions experienced specifically in response to trans gressive alcohol use.

VARIABLES OF THE STUDY

The variables selected for the present study are:

1. Guilt
2. Shame
3. Academic achievement

MEANING OF THE VARIABLES

Shame is often felt but little talked about and little understood. This is in part because it is so often confused with guilt, as if the two words were synonyms. It is also because the Biblical teaching on shame and its implications has been little developed by Christian theology.

To clarify the meaning of both words, let us look at their opposites. The opposite of guilt is innocence or moral purity. The opposite of shame, though, is not innocence; it is honour and glory. Think of Hosea 4:7, "... I will change their glory into shame," or Philippians 3:19, "... they glory in their shame." Shame is related to dishonour. Both shame and guilt are falling short of some standard, the subjective experience being the feeling of unacceptability and badness. Guilt is clearly for violating a rule, law or commandment. It is solidly in a moral framework, but from where, then, does shame come? What standard is violated when we experience shame?

If we look at three kinds of relationships between guilt and shame, the definition will become clearer. First of all, guilt and shame can come together for the same act. For example, I can tell a lie and feel guilt because I know it is wrong, but also feel shame because I had thought I was a strong enough person to have told the truth. Secondly, guilt and shame can function independently of each other. This goes both ways. I can know that I have done the wrong thing morally, but I can be quite unashamed about it. This is not to my credit, but it happens. In the same way I can feel shame for all kinds of things that are morally irrelevant. I can feel shame for being poor, for having been to the wrong kind of college or for having read or not read certain books. One area where most people feel shame is about their bodies. They feel ashamed of what they look like. In no sense are these moral problems or even moral issues. They are morally neutral, and yet we can experience extreme and painful shame over them. The third kind of relationship between guilt and shame is that of opposition: the two can work against each other. In other words, we can feel shame for doing the right thing, or sense a certain glory in doing the wrong thing. For example, in the Bible we are warned against being ashamed of Christ. We usually do not see the psychological implications of this. Believing and being identified with Jesus Christ is the most morally right thing we can do - and yet we can feel ashamed of doing it.

GUILT FEELINGS

Consider amoral psychopathic Mary. While she believes that it is morally wrong to steal a book from the library that consideration does not motivate her at all and she steals a book without regret or concern. She has no guilt feelings about her action even though she feels that she is guilty of stealing and so in that respect feels as if she is guilty. It appears to Mary that she is guilty of acting wrongly.

If that were enough for Mary to have guilt feelings, many but not all of the views mentioned in the previous section of this paper would be trivially true. Moral principles are trivially principles that one is guilty of violating if one violates them. If one knows one has acted wrongly, one is trivially warranted in feeling that one is guilty of having acted wrongly.

Obviously, psychopaths like Mary would be trivially susceptible to guilt feelings of this sort as long as they were able in this sense to feel that they were guilty of doing something morally wrong.

So, let us assume that guilt feelings are not simply feeling that one is guilty of something, but involve something more. What more?

Nontrivial guilt feelings have to be real feelings-with affect-indeed, with negative effect. To feel guilt is to feel bad.

They may involve agent regret, but that by itself is not enough for guilt. One regrets many things one has done without feeling guilty about them. For example, one may regret having moved one's queen to a particular square in a game of chess.

GUILT AT EACH LEVEL

Multiple sets of empirical research findings on guilt are reviewed to evaluate the view that guilt should be understood as an essentially social phenomenon that happens between people as much as it happens inside them. Guilt appears to arise from interpersonal transactions (including transgressions and positive inequities) and to vary significantly with the interpersonal context. In particular, guilt patterns appear to be strongest, most common, and most consistent in the context of communal relationships, which are characterized by expectations of mutual concern. Guilt serves various relationship-enhancing functions, including motivating people to treat partners well and avoid transgressions, minimizing inequities and enabling less powerful partners to get their way, and redistributing emotional distress.

DEFINITION OF GUILT

Meehan et al projection is another defensive tool with wide applications. It may take the form of blaming the victim: The victim of someone else's accident or bad luck may be offered criticism, the theory being that the victim may be at fault for having attracted the other person's hostility. Alternatively, not the guilt, but the condemning agency itself, may be projected onto other people, in the hope that they will look upon one's deeds more favorably than one's own conscience (a process that verges on ideas of reference).

Stuewig, & Mashek Sharing a feeling of guilt, and thereby being less alone with it, is a motive force in both art and joke-telling; while it is also possible to "borrow" a sense of guilt from someone who is seen as in the wrong, and thereby assuage one's own. Self-harm may be used as an alternative to compensating the object of one's transgression – perhaps in the form of not allowing oneself to enjoy opportunities open to one, or benefits due, as a result of uncompensated guilt feelings.

SHAME AT EACH LEVEL

The feeling of shame can be described as a sense of smallness, worthlessness, and powerlessness in a given situation. This is compounded by a simultaneous sense of feeling quite exposed and extremely concerned about the other's evaluation of oneself. In fact, shame can be defined as the emotional experience of another's scorn, real or imagined. The "self-in-the-eyes-of-the-other" is the focal point of shame- "I am as I am seen". This tends to produce an implosion of the body: head lowered, eyes closed / hidden, and the upper body curved in on itself as if trying to be as small as possible. The aversion of eye contact in such moments is easily understandable and to push for eye contact in moments of shame can actually be hurtful. Shame is much more visually based than verbally, as people report primarily internal images of being "looked at". Shame also induces hyper vigilant scanning in the service of self-protection. Shame is more than a feeling. It is an entire organism state that affects multiple systems in the body. Shame operates at primitive levels below the reach of rational thought processes. Embarrassment and humiliation are common variants of shame. Shame compounds itself like compound interest; we are frequently ashamed of feeling ashamed.

DEFINITION OF SHAME

Eric Johnson, Lawrence and Charlotte Hoover Professor of Pastoral Care, Southern Baptist Theological Seminary; Director of the Society for Christian Psychology "This side of heaven, we all struggle with shame and guilt. Ed Welch has served the church well by writing a thorough, practical, Christ-centered treatment of this difficult subject. Your love for Jesus will be greatly increased as you reflect on the way His work on the cross has freed you from the paralyzing effects of sin." Steve Viars, Senior Pastor of Faith Baptist Church; author of Putting Your Past in Its Place: Moving Forward in Freedom and Forgiveness.

Steve Viars, Senior Pastor of Faith Baptist Church; author of Putting Your Past in Its Place: Moving Forward in Freedom and Forgiveness "In Shame Interrupted, Ed Welch reminds us that the gospel really is good news. He provides a candid perspective on the suffocating reality of human shame with an honest courage that is only possible because of Christ's healing love. Dr. Welch brings the wisdom of an experienced counselor and the resilient hope of a Christ follower into this compassionate book."

Mark R. McMinn, PhD, Author of Sin and Grace in Christian Counseling "Dr. Welch seems to know what the reader needs long before he or she knows and recognizes that shamed people are often hopeless people. Shame Interrupted is not just a remedy for persons caught in paralyzing shame; it gives them hope that it is possible to live a life that feels clean and holy. That is a gift."

OPERATIONAL DEFINITIONS

Guilt

Guilt is a feeling of regret for having committed a mistake caused by conscience.

Shame

Shame is a state of disgrace it's when you do not want to see anyone face to face.

NEED FOR THE STUDY

Guilt can be healthy in that it is the feeling we experience when we do something we judge, by our moral code, to be wrong. It can also occur in many people just by having the urge to do something that they believe is wrong, or even by having a thought about committing an act of wrongdoing. Healthy guilt tends to keep us to socially acceptable pathways and functioning as useful individuals. It can help our ability to work hard and to be careful and kind. Guilt could be defined as our conscience. However, it should be noted that this 'conscience' is not always a reliable arbiter of 'good and bad' as it can only click in when we are aware of doing something wrong and is quite capable of making itself known when the misdeed is very minor or even appears inconsequential to the majority of people.

Shame is sometimes confused with guilt but can be defined as either the discomfort experienced when we don't live up to the expectations of others – the remorse and/or embarrassment experienced when we perceive that we have let others down and expect (or receive) their scorn or ridicule. This might be by breaching rules of good taste and/or tactful and acceptable behaviour in certain social situations. A second definition of shame is to do with self-disapproval. In the first definition, our shame might not occur if we were able to hide our anti-social or foolish acts from others, but with self-disapproval it is irrelevant whether others know or not; this type of shame might draw in embarrassment and make us feel ridiculous, inexcusably inadequate, contemptible, defective, disgraced, dishonourable…the list goes on. Shame of the self-disapproving kind can be very powerful and very destructive. A third element of shame, 'personal/original shame' will be looked at later in this booklet.

SCOPE OF THE STUDY

Guilt is the fact of being responsible for the commission of an offense. Guilt is composed of negative emotions related to wrongdoings or perceived failures to act appropriately. Guilt includes feelings of sorrow, repentance, and disappointment in one's actions. Guilt is both a cognitive and an emotional experience that occurs when a person realizes that he or she has violated a moral standard and is responsible for that violation. A guilty conscience results from thoughts that we have not lived up to our ideal self. Shame is a painful emotion arising from the knowing (consciousness) of something dishonourable, improper, ridiculous, disgraceful, embarrassing, etc, done by oneself or another.

Shame is directly attributed to feeling guilty about something, hence shame and guilt intertwine. Shame consists of a negative evaluation of one's own worth, because he or she has acted "wrongly." Shame is conceptualized as including feelings of disgrace, disrepute, dishonour, loss of self-esteem, loss of virtue, and loss of personal integrity.

IMPORTANCE OF THE STUDY

Succeeding or failing to meet the standards, rules, and goals of one's group or society determines how well an individual forms relationships with other members of the group. Living up to one's own internalized set of standards or failing to live up to them is the basis of complex emotions. The so-called self-conscious emotions, such as guilt, pride, shame, and hubris, require a fairly sophisticated level of intellectual development. To feel them, individuals must have a sense of self as well as a set of standards. They must also have notions of what constitutes success and failure, and the capacity to evaluate their own behaviour.

Self-conscious emotions are difficult to study. For one thing, there are no clear elicitors of these emotions. Joy registers predictably on a person's face at the approach of a friend, and caution appears at the approach of a stranger. But what situation is guaranteed to elicit pride or shame, guilt or embarrassment? These emotions are so dependent on a person's own experience, expectations, and culture, that it is difficult to design uniform experiments.

STATEMENT OF THE PROBLEM

"Guilt and Shame on Academic achievement among Higher Secondary School Students" is chosen for the study."

Sample

The focus for this study is on higher secondary students. Convenient random sampling technique is used for the selection of the sample. Total of 300 students were randomly selected from three different types of schools in Thiruvallur district. The investigator selected 100 students' 50 boys and 50 girls from Government school, 100 students 50 boys and 50 girls from Government Aided School and 100 students 50 boys and 50 girls from Private school.

Objectives

- To relate Guilt with that of Shame of the sample.
- To find out the impact of gender on Guilt and Shame of the sample.
- To find out the association between Guilt with that of parents qualification, occupation, annual income and types of family.

- To find out the association between Shame with that of parents qualification, father occupation, annual income and types of family.
- To inter relate Academic Achievement with Guilt and Shame of the sample.

DELIMITATION OF THE STUDY

- This study was limited to 3 types of (Government, Government-Aided and Private) schools in (Thiruvallur District) Only.
- This sample was limited to 300 students of XI standard only.
- This study was restricted to the variables Guilt and Shame on Academic Achievement for the study.

❐

2

Review of Related Literature

Study of related literature implies location, reading and evaluating reports of researches as well as reports of casual conservation and opinions that are related to the investigators planed research project. According to Best and Khan (1936) a summary or the writing of recognized authorities and of previous research provides evidence that the research was familiar with what is already known and what is still unknown and untested. Since the effective research is based upon past knowledge, this step helps to eliminate the duplication of what has been done and provides useful hypothesis and helpful suggestions for significant investigation.

NEED AND IMPORTANCE OF REVIEW OF RELATED LITERATURE

Research is not an isolated activity but part of an ongoing and concentrated effort to attain and understand the reality. Thus every attempt to un earth truth is connected with all such endeavors of the past and elsewhere therefore it is imperative that the researcher takes pain to find what his fellow researchers in other parts of the worked has done in the field of his or her research.

The survey of related literature is a crucial aspect of the planning of the study and the time spent in such, surely is a wise investment. Hence an attempt has made to review the studies related to the present study conducted in India and abroad.

REVIEWS RELATED TO GUILT

Used semi projective and scenario-based measures to identify evidence for adaptive or maladaptive aspects of guilt and shame in 5- to 12-year olds. Found that shame and projective guilt were related to symptoms as rated by parents, self-blame, and attempts to minimize painful feelings. Scenario-based guilt was related to fewer symptoms in boys but greater symptoms in girls (Ferguson et al 1999).

Explores how gender role stress variables are related to shame-proneness, guilt-proneness, and externalization. Analyses revealed three significant roots for the male sample accounting for 50% of the total variance between gender role stress and self-conscious emotions, and 1 significant root for the female sample accounting for 31% of the variance. (Efthim et al 2001).

In the study examined guilt feelings among social work students who were pregnant for the first time during field work training. Semi-structured interviews were conducted either in the 9th month (n=5) or 2-12 months after delivery (n=5). Content analysis revealed 6 main triggers, illustrated by excerpts, which stimulated field students' guilt feelings. Discussion of the results focused on the types of guilt described (omnipotent, separation, outdoing/survivor), manifestations of shame, and diverse possible explanations for the field students' guilt feelings, along with implications for social work supervision and practice. (Baum et al 2006).

Facial composite research has generally focused on the investigative utility of composites--using composites to find suspects. However, almost no work has examined the diagnostic utility of facial composites--the extent to which composites can be used as evidence against a suspect. For example, detectives and jurors may use the perceived similarity of a suspect to a composite as evidence to determine the likelihood of a suspect's guilt. However, research in social cognition and models of cognitive coherence suggest that these similarity judgments may be biased by evaluators' pre-existing beliefs of guilt. Two studies examined how pre-existing beliefs of guilt influence similarity ratings between a suspect and a facial composite. Study 1 (n = 93) demonstrated that mock-investigators' beliefs in a suspect's guilt inflated their subsequent similarity ratings. Study 2 (n = 49) demonstrated that mock-jurors' beliefs in a defendant's guilt predicted their similarity ratings. These findings highlight a problem of using facial composites as evidence against a suspect, and demonstrate the malleability of similarity judgments. (Charman et al 2009).

Recent theoretical and empirical work has facilitated the drawing of sharp conceptual distinctions between shame and guilt. A clear view of these distinctions has permitted development of a research literature aimed at evaluating the differential associations of shame and guilt with depressive symptoms. This study quantitatively summarized the magnitude of associations of shame and guilt with depressive symptoms. Two hundred forty-two effect sizes were obtained from 108 studies employing 22,411 participants. Shame showed significantly stronger associations with depressive symptoms (r = 0.43) than guilt (r = 0.28). However, the association of shame and depressive symptoms was statistically indistinguishable from the associations of 2 maladaptive variants of guilt and depressive symptoms ("contextual-maladaptive" guilt, involving exaggerated responsibility for uncontrollable events, r = 0.39; generalized guilt, involving "free-floating" guilt divorced from specific contexts, r = 0.42). Other factors also moderated the effects. "External shame", which involves negative views of self as seen through the eyes of others, was associated with larger effect sizes (r = 0.56) than "internal shame" (r = 0.42), which involves negative views of self as seen through one's own eyes. Depressive symptom measures that invoked the term guilt yielded stronger associations between guilt and depressive symptoms (r = 0.33) than depressive symptom measures that did not (r = 0.21). Age, sex, and ethnicity (proportion of Whites to Asians) did not moderate the effects. Although these correlation data are ambiguous with respect to their causal interpretation, results suggest that shame should figure more prominently in understandings of the emotional underpinnings of depressive symptoms (Kim et al 2011).

In this two studies investigated body guilt (i.e., feeling regret and remorse over how the body looks and a desire for reparative action to "fix" the body) within the framework of objectification theory among predominantly White British undergraduate women. In Study 1 (N = 225), participants completed self-report measures of interpersonal sexual objectification, self-surveillance, body shame, body guilt, and eating restraint. Path analyses indicated support for the inclusion of body guilt in the objectification model, with body shame and body guilt fully mediating the relationship between self-surveillance and eating restraint. In Study 2 (N = 85), participants reported higher body guilt, self-surveillance, body shame, and eating restraint when self-objectification was situational activated, compared to the activation of body empowerment or a neutral condition. Path analyses in the second study replicated the objectification model from Study 1 with a state measure of self-objectification. These findings suggest that women also feel guilt (in addition to shame) about their bodies when attention is directed toward their physical appearance and wish to "correct" their body via disordered eating. Acknowledging women's feelings of guilt in relation to not meeting restrictive beauty standards furthers our understanding of women's experience of objectification and provides an additional target for reducing women's mental health risks (Calogero et al 2011).

Explored forgiving and its relationship to adaptive moral emotional processes: proneness to shame; guilt; anger; and empathic responsiveness. Gender differences associated with forgiving were analyzed. Participants were 138 graduate students in an urban university. Results revealed that guilt-proneness was positively related to Total Forgiveness, as were Empathetic Concern and Perspective Taking. (Sara et al 2011).

The purpose of the present study was to examine the relation between narcissistic orientations (grandiose sense of self-importance, interpersonal exploitation, and narcissistic rage) and relational aggression (self-satisfactory and punishment type) and the mediating effects of guilt feelings toward and perceived classroom norms against relational aggression. The sample consisted of 240 5th-grade and 6th-grade students (10- to 12-years-old) from two public elementary schools and 307 7th-, 8th-, and 9th-grade students (12- to 15-years-old) from two public middle schools in Japan. Results of structural equation modelling demonstrated that narcissistic rage was positively associated with relate anal aggression (punishment type). Moreover, interpersonal exploitation was related to more relational aggression (self-satisfactory and punishment type); however, guilt feelings toward and perceived classroom norms against relational aggression mediated this association. Age and gender did not largely affect these effects. Social and developmental processes involving relational aggression, narcissistic orientations, and guilt feelings and perceived classroom norms were discussed (Onishi et al 2012).

Divorce is often accompanied by feelings of guilt toward the former spouse. So far, no scale has been available to measure such feelings. For this purpose, the authors developed the Guilt in Separation Scale (GISS). Content validity was assured by using experts and lay experts to generate and select items. Exploratory analyses were run on samples of 214 divorced individuals and confirmatory analyses on 458 individuals who were in the process of divorcing. Evidence was proved for the reliability and construct validity of the GISS. The internal consistency was high ([alpha] = 0.91), as were the 6-month and 12-month test-retest reliabilities (r = 0.72 and r = 0.76, respectively). The GISS was related to shame, regret and compassion, locus of cause of the separation, unfaithfulness, and psychological functioning. (Ann et al 2012).

Divorce is often accompanied by feelings of guilt toward the former spouse. So far, no scale has been available to measure such feelings. For this purpose, the authors developed the Guilt in Separation Scale (GISS). Content validity was assured by using experts and lay experts to generate and select items. Exploratory analyses were run on samples of 214 divorced individuals and confirmatory analyses on 458 individuals who were in the process of divorcing. Evidence was proved for the reliability and construct validity of the GISS.

The internal consistency was high ([alpha] = 0.91), as were the 6-month and 12-month test-retest reliabilities (r = 0.72 and r = 0.76, respectively). The GISS was related to shame, regret, and compassion, locus of cause of the separation, unfaithfulness, and psychological functioning. (Wietzker et al 2012).

REVIEWS RELATED TO SHAME

In this study focuses on the prediction of self-initiated bullying from family, school, personality, and shame management variables. Reiterative shaming theory proved a theoretical framework for data gathered from students (n = 1,401) and their parents (n = 978). To test the importance of shame management in relation to bullying, the MOSS-SASD instrument (Management of Shame State-Shame Acknowledgment and Shame Displacement) was developed. Bullying was related to a child's unacknowledged shame and its displacement to other-directed blame and anger. The results of path analysis indicated that shame management partially mediated the effects of family, school, and personality variables on bullying. The implications of these findings for creating a safer school environment are discussed. (Ahmed et al 2004).

When faced with shame, children can either respond in submissive ways to withdraw from their environment or in externalizing ways to oppose their environment. This study tested the hypothesis that fragile-positive views of self predispose children to respond in externalizing ways to shame situations. Narcissism, actual and perceived social preference, global self-worth and propensity towards externalizing shame responding were measured in 122 pre-adolescent children. As expected, results revealed that narcissism, in contrast to global self-worth, was associated with externalizing shame responding. In addition, actual but not perceived social preference was inversely related to externalizing shame responding, suggesting that the social self-perceptions of children prone to employ externalizing shame responses may be inflated. Discussion focuses on the self-regulatory function of externalizing shame responses. (Tjeert et al 2007).

Although shame plays a vital role in psychosocial functioning and development, it has also been implicated in several mental health problems, such as depression, suicidal behaviour, and posttraumatic stress disorder. Given the potentially debilitating impact of shame on adjustment, an understanding of resilience in the face of this emotion is essential. The purpose of this study was to explore how adults bounce back from significant shame experiences, based on the subjective perspectives of participants. Interviews were conducted with 13 adults who recalled events or situations that elicited intense feelings of shame. Grounded theory was used in the collection and analysis of the data. In the findings, shame is conceptualized as an assault on the self, where the individual's self-concept, social connection, and sense of power and control come under attack. Individuals bounce back from this adversity through a process of self-reconstruction. This process is represented by the core category rebuilding of the self and by 5 interrelated subcategories, including connecting, refocusing, accepting, understanding, and resisting. Implications for counselling and directions for further research are discussed (Van Vliet et al 2008).

To examine whether shame-proneness mediates the relationship between women's histories of childhood sexual abuse and their current partner and family conflict and child maltreatment. Previous research has found that women with childhood sexual abuse histories experience heightened shame and interpersonal conflict. However, research examining the relationship of shame to interpersonal conflict is lacking. Method: Participants were 129 mothers of children enrolled in a summer camp program for at-risk children from financially disadvantaged families. Data were collected on women's childhood abuse histories, shame in daily life, and current interpersonal conflict involving family conflict, intimate partner conflict (verbal and physical aggression), and child maltreatment. Results: consistent with our hypothesis, the results of hierarchical regressions and logistic regression indicated that shame significantly mediated the association between childhood sexual abuse and interpersonal conflict. Women with sexual abuse histories reported more shame in their daily lives, which in turn was associated with higher levels of conflicts with intimate partners (self-verbal aggression and partner-physical aggression) and in the family. Shame did not mediate the relationship between mothers' histories of sexual abuse and child maltreatment. Conclusion: The role of shame in the intimate partner and family conflicts of women with sexual abuse histories has not been examined. The current findings indicate that childhood sexual abuse was related to interpersonal conflicts indirectly through the emotion of shame. Practical Implications: These findings highlight the importance of investigating the role of shame in the interpersonal conflicts of women with histories of childhood sexual abuse. Healthcare professionals in medical and mental health settings frequently treat women with abuse histories who are involved in family and partner conflicts. Assessing and addressing the links of abused women's shame to interpersonal conflicts could be important in clinical interventions. (Kim et al 2009).

The purpose of this study was to investigate coming out to family and friends and their relationships to shame, internalized heterosexist, lesbian identity, and perceived social support in Chinese lesbians from 2 different cultural settings--Mainland China (N = 244) and Hong Kong (N = 234). Results of structural equation modelling showed that, in both samples, a sense of shame was related to internalized heterosexist and a devaluation of one's lesbian identity, which in turn was related to a decreased likelihood of coming out to others. Shame was also associated with a reduced perception of support from friends, which seemed in turn to exacerbate internalized heterosexism among lesbians. Family support was generally unrelated to countess, except for countess to friends in the Hong Kong sample. Results are discussed in relation to the cultural stigma attached to same-sex orientation and the cultural practice of shaming that parents use to socialize children. (Sheung-Tak et al 2010).

Recent theoretical and empirical work has facilitated the drawing of sharp conceptual distinctions between shame and guilt. A clear view of these distinctions has permitted development of a research literature aimed at evaluating the differential associations of shame and guilt with depressive symptoms. This study quantitatively summarized the magnitude of associations of shame and guilt with depressive symptoms. Two hundred forty-two effect sizes were obtained from 108 studies employing 22,411 participants. Shame showed significantly stronger associations with depressive symptoms (r = 0.43) than guilt (r = 0.28). However, the association of shame and depressive symptoms was statistically indistinguishable from the associations of 2 maladaptive variants of guilt and depressive symptoms ("contextual-maladaptive" guilt, involving exaggerated responsibility for uncontrollable events, r = 0.39; generalized guilt, involving "free-floating" guilt divorced from specific contexts, r = 0.42). Other factors also moderated the effects. "External shame", which involves negative views of self as seen through the eyes of others, was associated with larger effect sizes (r = 0.56) than "internal shame" (r = 0.42), which involves negative views of self as seen through one's own eyes. Depressive symptom measures that invoked the term guilt yielded stronger associations between guilt and depressive symptoms (r = 0.33) than depressive symptom measures that did not (r = 0.21). Age, sex, and ethnicity (proportion of Whites to Asians) did not moderate the effects. Although these correlation data are ambiguous with respect to their causal interpretation, results suggest that shame should figure more prominently in understandings of the emotional underpinnings of depressive symptoms. (Randall S. et al 2011).

The current study examined the moderating role of shame proneness on the association between physical, psychological, and sexual intimate partner violence victimization and depressive and anxious symptoms among male and female college students (N = 967). Students completed self-report measures of dating violence, depression, anxiety, and shame proneness. Results showed that shame proneness moderated the association between all forms of victimization and mental health symptoms. A three-way interaction revealed that sexual victimization predicted symptoms of anxiety to a greater extent for men than for women at high levels of shame proneness. Furthermore, results showed that gender moderated the association between physical and psychological victimization and health outcomes, such that victimization was related to increased depressive and anxious symptoms for men but not for women. Interpretations of these findings are discussed in relation to violence interventions, including primary prevention, and men's health. (Shorey et al 2011).

This study explored the association of shame and guilt with PTSD among women who had experienced intimate partner violence (IPV). Sixty-three women were assessed by a research clinic serving the mental health needs of women IPV survivors. Results indicated that shame, guilt-related distress, and guilt-related cognitions showed significant associations with PTSD but global guilt did not. When shame and guilt were examined in the context of specific forms of psychological abuse, moderation analyses indicated that high levels of both emotional/verbal abuse and dominance/isolation interacted with high levels of shame in their association with PTSD. Neither guilt-related distress nor guilt-related cognitions were moderated by specific forms of psychological abuse in their association with PTSD. These data support the conceptualization of shame, guilt distress, and guilt cognitions as relevant features of PTSD. Results are discussed in light of proposed changes to diagnostic criteria for PTSD. (J. Houston et al 2011).

Research evidence is accumulating to suggest that shame can be implicated in important ways in student adjustment to the learning environment. Student survey data spring-fall 2010 suggest that shame is associated with variables thought to be closely related to student learning--sense of community, burnout and achievement goals--and underline the significance of what Nathan son has called the compass of shame in understanding students' struggles with shame. The paper closes with suggestions from the literature on dealing with student shame in the classroom and in academic advising. (Diane Elizabeth et al 2012).

Theorists, clinicians, and researchers have suggested that shame is a central concern in the lives of sexual minority individuals. Cognitive theorists believe that shame occurs when a person fails to achieve his or her standards, which are often based on social, cultural, and spiritual values. Although it is asserted that stigma causes shame among members of a sexual minority, the empirical evidence suggests that negative internal cognitions are partly responsible. By targeting negative beliefs, counsellors can help sexual minorities reduce their sense of shame, particularly around issues related to sexual identity. The authors offer counselling strategies for reducing shame in sexual minority clients (Mark a et al 2013).

REVIEWS RELATED TO ACADEMIC ACHIEVEMENT

An investigation was conducted to find the relationship between some environmental factor and academic achievement. The investigation reveals that the environmental level includes parent's education, their occupational states, socio economics level and caste system (Ahuluwalia and Gupta 1968).

A study was conducted on measured intelligence and Academic achievement as related to cultural atmosphere in the home. The study reveals that better educated parents take greater interest in better children studies. The cultural atmosphere of the homes of the pupils influences their academic achievement (Chopra 1970).

In his study explains that new parents as teacher reveal that if parents want to provide optional facilities environment conductive to the cognitive development of their children. They should play important role in the educational process of their children. (Mize.J.C 1978).

It was conducted that inherited differences in ability, initial levels of ability, the quality of schooling available, ability, family, physical resources, differences in home educational learning environment are some of the most obvious sources of contribution to the difference in academic achievement among children. (Fotheringam and Creal 1980).

The relationship of parent's support to children's school achievement. The study reveals that parents should provide active support of their children and have better relationship with their children contribute more to their children's success than to those who provide passive support (Watson et al., 1983).

A study was conducted on parent involvement and Commerce Achievement: Contrast Across Racial and Ethnic Groups found that close parent – teenage relationship was one of the major ways in which minority (except Hispanic) families positively influenced Commerce outcome.(Wenfan Yan and Lin Quiyun 1988).

A study was conducted on Parents participation in children's Academic Activities in relation to their Academic achievement at primary level. The study research that commonly parents do not realize the significance of their participation in children's academic activities. Significant influence on the child's personality is mostly related to parent's outcome of all influences. And most influencing factor of educational interference or the academic achievement in commerce. (Agarwal 1998)

In this study Parental Involvement and student Achievement a Meta Analysis indicate that the academic achievement score distribution or range of scores for children whose parents were highly involved in their education was substantially higher than that of their counter parts whose parents were less involved. (Keynes. H. 2005).

CONCLUSION

Survey of related studies consists of searching, identifying, studying and evaluating report of relevant researchers; it is an effort to get one familiarize with all that has been done in a particular area of research. It provides ideas, theories, explanations, hypotheses or methods of research which are valuable in formulating and studying the problem. It prevents pointless repetition of research. Above all it contributes to the general scholarship of the investigator. ❐

3

Design of the Study

Research design is needed because it facilities the smooth sailing of the various research operations, thereby making research as efficient as possible yielding maximal information with minimal expenditure of effort, time and money.

This chapter elaborates the design of the study, psychological tools used for study, nature selection of the sample, a brief description of the procedure adopted for the collection of data for its scoring and classification finally the proposed statistical treatment of the data for testing the hypothesis that were formulated is explained.

SAMPLE

A convenient random sampling technique was adapted for the selection of sample. Total of 300 students were randomly selected from three different types of schools in Thiruvallur district. The investigator selected 100 students' (50 boys and 50 girls) from Government school, 100 students (50 boys and 50 girls) from Government Aided School and 100 students (50 boys and 50 girls) from Private school.

Distribution of the Sample

Type of school	School Name	Gender		Sample
		Boys	Girls	
Government	G.H.S.S Kannigaipeir	50	50	100
Government aided	St.Mary's Higher Secondary School	50	50	100
Private school	J.N.N Matriculation Higher Secondary School	50	50	100

STATEMENT OF THE PROBLEM

"Guilt and Shame on Academic Achievement among Higher Secondary School Students" is the topic chosen for the study.

LIMITATIONS

1. The study could be extended to college Students.
2. Similar study comprising different districts can be attempted.
3. It can be done by including more number of schools students.

OBJECTIVES

1. To relate Guilt with that of Shame of the sample.
2. To find out the impact of gender on Guilt and Shame of the sample.
3. To find out the association between Guilt with that of parents qualification, occupation, annual income and types of family.
4. To find out the association between Shame with that of parents qualification, father occupation, annual income and types of family.
5. To inter relate Academic Achievement with Guilt and Shame of the sample.

HYPOTHESES

1. There are no significant differences between Guilt of boys and girls from the total sample
2. There are no significant differences between Shame of boys and girls from the total sample
3. There are no significant differences between Academic Achievement of boys and girls from the total sample
4. There is no significant relationship between Guilt and shame
5. There is no significant relationship between Guilt and academic achievement
6. There is no significant relationship between academic achievement and shame
7. Type of family does not associate with Guilt
8. Education of father does not associate with Guilt

9. Education of mother does not associate with Guilt
10. Occupation of father does not associate with Guilt
11. Occupation of mother does not associate with Guilt.
12. Annual income does not associate with Guilt
13. Type of family does not associate with Shame
14. Education of father does not associate with Shame
15. Education of mother does not associate with Shame
16. Occupation of father does not associate with Shame.
17. Occupation of mother does not associate with Shame
18. Annual income does not associate with Shame

RESEARCH TOOLS SELECTED FOR THE PRESENT STUDY

The following tools have been used by the investigator to carry out this study.

1. Personal data sheet developed by the investigator
2. Guilt scale Taya R. Cohen (April 2011)
3. Shame scale Ed Diner et al (1985)

GUILT SCALE

Description

Taya R. Cohen (April 2011) has been used in order to find the level of Guilt of students. The scale consists of 10 items and all of these items are positive. The Guilt Questionnaire assesses two dimensions of Guilt using 10 items rated on a seven-point scale from "Absolutely True" to "Absolutely Untrue." The Presence of Meaning subscale measures how full respondents feel their lives are of meaning. The Search for Meaning subscale measures how engaged and motivated respondents are in efforts to find meaning or deepen their understanding of meaning in their lives. The MLQ has good reliability, test-retest stability, stable factor structure, and convergence among informants. Presence is positively related to well-being, intrinsic religiosity, extraversion and agreeableness, and negatively related to anxiety and depression. Search is positively related to religious quest, rumination, past-negative and present-fatalistic time perspectives, negative effect, depression, and neuroticism, and negatively related to future time perspective, close-mindedness (dogmatism), and well-being. Presence relates as expected with personal growth self-appraisals, and altruistic and spiritual behaviours as assessed through daily diaries. The MLQ takes about 5 minutes to complete.

Administration

Students were asked to sit comfortably and fill their general data on the data sheet given. Even though there was no time limit to finish the Questionnaire, students completed the task within 30 minutes. They were also told that their responses would be kept confidential and will be used only for the purpose of research.

Scoring Procedure of Guilt

The weight age of 7, 6, 5, 4, 3, 2 and 1 are given for the categories 'Very unlikely, Unlikely, Slightly Unlikely, About 50%, Likely 50%, Slightly, Likely, Likely and Very likely ' respectively. The score of an individual with respect to Guilt is the sum of all scores in each of the 8 items.

For positive Questionnaire scorings are

Very unlikely	-	7
Unlikely	-	6
Slightly Unlikely	-	5
About 50%, Likely 50%	-	4
Slightly, Likely	-	3
Likely	-	2
Very Likely	-	1

Reliability

Reliability of Guilt scale was established using split-half method. The reliability was computed and it was found to be (0.93).

Validity

The index of validity, which is the square root of reliability and it, was found to be (0.96). Hence the tool is valid for the present study.

SHAME SCALE

Description

ED Diener et al (1985) Life Shame scale has been used in order to find the level of subjective happiness of students. The scale consists 5 items. The Shame Scale was developed to assess satisfaction with people's lives as a whole. The scale does not assess satisfaction with specific life domains, such as health or finances, but allows subjects to integrate and weigh these domains in whatever way they choose. It takes only a few minutes to complete.

Administration

Students were asked to sit comfortably and fill their general data on the data sheet given. Even though there was no time limit to finish the Questionnaire, students completed the task within 20 minutes. They were also told that their responses would be kept confidential and will be used only for the purpose of research.

Scoring Procedure of Shame

The weightage of 7, 6, 5, 4, 3, 2 and 1 are given for the categories 'Very unlikely, Unlikely, Slightly Unlikely, About 50%, Likely 50%, Slightly Likely, Likely Very Likely' respectively. The score of an individual with respect to Shame is the sum of all scores in each of the 8 items.

For Questionnaire scorings are

Very unlikely	-	7
Unlikely	-	6
Slightly Unlikely	-	5
About 50%, Likely 50%	-	4
Slightly, Likely	-	3
Likely	-	2
Very Likely	-	1

Reliability

Reliability of Shame scale was established using split-half method. The reliability was computed and it was found to be (0.81).

Validity

The index of validity, which is the square root of reliability and it, was found to be (0.9).

Personal Data Sheet

The personal data sheet was prepared to collect information on personal details such us gender, type of school, type of family, father/mother qualifications, father/mother occupation, Annual Income.

Pilot Study

Pilot study was carried out to know the suitability of the time of required administering the Guilt and to establish the reliability and validity of the tools. 50 students were selected for the pilot study. The tools were given. Based on the data, reliability and validity of the tools questionnaire were calculated for the present study.

Academic Achievement

The investigator procured quarterly examination marks of the higher secondary students from teachers of three types of schools (Government, Government Aided, private) to do my thesis.

Statistical Analyses

Suitable descriptive and inferential statistical techniques were used in the interpretation of data to draw out a meaningful picture of results from the collected data. In the present study, the following statistics measures were used,

1. Descriptive Analysis
2. Differential Analysis
3. Relational Analysis
4. Chi-square Analysis

i. MEAN

$$\text{Mean } (\bar{X}) = A + \frac{\sum fd}{\sum a} \times i$$

Where,

A = Assumed Mean

f = Frequency

d = Deviation from the Assumed Mean

i = Class Interval

ii. STANDARD DEVIATION

$$SD(\sigma) = \sqrt{\frac{Efd^2}{N} = \left[\frac{Efd}{N}\right]^2} \times i$$

Where,

f = Frequency

d = Deviation for the Assumed Mean

i = Class Interval

N = Total Frequency

iii. 't' Test

To compare the significant to different between means of various measures 't' test is used 't' ratio is calculated from the relation.

$$\text{'T'-ratio} = \frac{M_1 \sim M_2}{\sqrt{\frac{\sigma_1^2}{N_1} + \frac{\sigma_2^2}{N_2}}}$$

M_1, M_2 = Difference between the Means

σ_1, σ_1 = Standard Deviation

N_1, N_2 = Total Number of Items

iv. CO-EFFICIENT OF CORRELATION (r)

$$r = \frac{n\sum XY - \sum x - \sum Y}{\sqrt{\left[N\sum X^2 - \left(\sum X\right)^2\right]}\sqrt{\left[N\sum Y^2 - \left(\sum Y\right)^2\right]}}$$

XY – Variables

N – Total Strength

v. CHI – SQUARE DISTRIBUTION

$$x^2 = \frac{\sum (f_o - f_e)^2}{f_e}$$

DF = (r –1) x (c – 1)

fo = Observed Frequency

fe = Excepted Frequency

CONCLUSION

Adopting the methods and the procedure discussed earlier in this chapter, tests were administered and scored. The obtained data were then analyzed using appropriate statistical techniques. The next chapter presents the analysis and interpretation of the data collected in the light of the hypotheses formulated.

❐

4

Analysis and Interpretation of Data

Any research work could be meaningful when the data were analyzed and interpreted properly. Therefore, the researcher has given much importance to this part. The data collected from the sample analyzed and interpreted in the following heads.

- Descriptive analysis
- Differential analysis

DESCRIPTIVE ANALYSIS

It includes comparison of measures of central tendency such as the mean and the measures of variability such as standard deviation. The calculated values are used to describe the properties of the different sub-samples.

DIFFERENTIAL ANALYSIS

It contains the determinations of the statistical significance of the difference between groups with reference to selected variables. It contains 't' test. A 't' test is a numerical procedure that takes into account the difference between the means of the two sub-groups the size of the sample in each group and amount of variation of spread present in the scores. Thus the 't' test is a technique to find out whether the difference the mean performance of the two groups is significant or not.

Hypothesis-1

There are no significant differences between guilt of Boys and Girls from the total sample

TABLE. 4.1: Differentiation of Guilt in Boys and Girls from Government School.

Variable	Gender	N	Mean	S.D	C.R	L.S
Guilt	Boys	50	57.69	6.89	1.004	N.S
	Girls	50	59.33	9.69		

N.S- Not Significant

TABLE. 4.2: Differentiation of guilt Boys and Girls from Government Aided School.

Variable	Gender	N	Mean	S.D	C.R	L.S
Guilt	Boys	50	61.33	7.38	1.076	N.S
	Girls	50	60.08	3.63		

N.S- Not Significant

TABLE.4.3: Differentiation of guilt Boys and Girls from Private School.

Variable	Gender	N	Mean	S.D	C.R	L.S
Guilt	Boys	50	63.65	6.27	1.982	0.05
	Girls	50	61.45	4.67		

From the table 3 from figure D it is understood that the calculated 'Critical Ratio' values are more than that of table 'Critical Ratio' values. Hence the hypothesis is rejected and proved that there is significant difference between guilt of boys and girls of Private School from the total sample.

From the table 1 and 2 and also from figure B and C it is understood that the calculated 'Critical Ratio' values are less than that of table 'Critical Ratio' values. Hence the hypothesis is accepted and proved that there is no significant difference between guilt of boys and girls of Government and Government Aided from the total sample.

Hypothesis -2

There are no significant differences between Shame of Boys and Girls from the total sample

TABLE. 4.4: Differentiations of Shame Boys and Girls from Government School.

Variable	Gender	N	Mean	S.D	C.R	L.S
Shame	Boys	50	52.39	7.06		
	Girls	50	54.98	10.05	1.49	N.S

N.S - Not Significant

TABLE.4.5: Differentiations of Shame Boys and Girls from Government Aided School.

Variable	Gender	N	Mean	S.D	C.R	L.S
Shame	Boys	50	57.41	9.798		
	Girls	50	60.20	3.84	1.87	N.S

N.S - Not Significant

From the table 4 and 5 and also from figure E and F it is understood that the calculated 'Critical Ratio' values are less than that of table 'Critical Ratio' values. Hence the hypothesis is accepted and proved that there is no significant difference between Shame of boys and girls of Government and Government Aided from the total sample.

TABLE.4.6: Differentiations of Shame Boys and Girls from Private School.

Variable	Gender	N	Mean	S.D	C.R	L.S
Shame	Boys	50	56.35	6.25		
	Girls	50	61.33	7.199	3.69	0.01

From the table 6 from figure G it is understood that the calculated 'Critical Ratio' values are more than that of table 'Critical Ratio' values. Hence the hypothesis is rejected and proved that there is significant difference between Shame of boys and girls Private School from the total sample.

Hypothesis - 3

There are no significant differences between Academic achievement of Boys and Girls from the total sample.

TABLE.4.7: Differentiation of Academic achievement in Boys and Girls from government school.

Variable	Gender	N	Mean	S.D	C.R	L.S
Academic achievement	Boys	50	1056.63	75.13		
	Girls	50	1146.78	89.23	5.465	**0.01**

From the table 7 from figure J it is understood that the calculated 'Critical Ratio' values are more than that of table 'Critical Ratio' values. Hence the hypothesis is rejected and proved that there is significant difference between Academic achievement of boys and girls Government School from the total sample.

TABLE.4.8: Differentiation of Academic Achievement in Boys and Girls from Government Aided School.

Variable	Gender	N	Mean	S.D	C.R	L.S
Academic achievement	Boys	50	1124.35	137.05	1.803	N.S
	Girls	50	1162.70	61.94		

N.S- Not Significant

TABLE. 4.9: Differentiation of Academic Achievement in Boys and Girls from Private School.

Variable	Gender	N	Mean	S.D	C.R	L.S
Academic achievement	Boys	50	1741.69	82.36	0.491	N.S
	Girls	50	1750.59	102.67		

N.S- Not Significant

From the table 8 and 9 and also from figure H and I it is understood that the calculated 'Critical Ratio' values are less than that of table 'Critical Ratio' values. Hence the hypothesis is accepted and proved that there is no significant difference between Academic achievement of boys and girls Government Aided and Private school from the total sample.

Hypothesis - 4

There is no significant relationship between existing Guilt and Shame of the total sample.

TABLE. 4.10: Relationship between Guilt and Shame of the total sample.

Variable	Type of management	Gender	N	Correlation Coefficient	't'- test	L.S
Guilt and Shame.	**Government**	**Boys**	**50**	**0.1458**	**1.0931**	NS
		Girls	50	0.0385	0.272	NS
	Government Aided	Boys	50	0.3582	3.0979	0.01
		Girls	50	0.173	1.318	NS
	Private	Boys	50	0.179	1.3685	NS
		Girls	50	0.029	0.2039	NS

From the table 10, and also from figure K, In the case of boys and girls of Government, girls of Government aided and boys and girls of Private school, the calculated coefficient values were less than that table of correlation coefficient values. Hence the hypothesis is accepted and proved that there are no significant relationships between Guilt and Shame of the sample. In the case of government aided boys the calculated correlation coefficient values are more than that of table correlation coefficient values. Hence hypothesis is rejected and proved that there is significant relationship between Guilt and Shame in the case government aided boys.

Hypothesis - 5

There is no significant relationship existing between Guilt and Academic achievement of the total sample.

TABLE.4.11: Relationship between Guilt and Academic Achievement of the Total Sample

Variable	Type of management	Gender	N	Correlation Coefficient	't'- test	L.S
Guilt and Academic achievement	Government	Boys	50	- 0.2928	2.412	0.05
		Girls	50	- 0.0167	0.1167	NS
	Government Aided	Boys	50	- 0.0138	0.0963	NS
		Girls	50	- 0.0955	0.6957	NS
	Private	Boys	50	- 0.0251	0.176	NS
		Girls	50	- 0.2552	2.009	0.05

N.S – Not Significant

From the table 11, and also from figure L, In the case of girls of Government, boys and girls of Government aided and boys of Private school, the calculated coefficient values were less than that table of correlation coefficient values. Hence the hypothesis is accepted and proved that there are no significant relationships between Guilt and Academic achievement of the sample.

In the case of boys of Government school and girls of private school the calculated correlation coefficient values are more than that of table correlation coefficient values. Hence hypothesis is rejected and proved that there is significant relationship between Guilt and Academic Achievement in the case of boys of Government school and girls of private school.

Hypothesis - 6

There is no significant relationship existing between Academic achievement and Shame of the total sample

TABLE.4.12: Relationship between Shame and Academic Achievement of the Total Sample

Variable	Type of management	Gender	N	Correlation Coefficient	't'- test	L.S
Academic achievement and Shame	Government	Boys	50	- 0.0731	0.526	NS
		Girls	50	- 0.0416	0.2944	NS
	Government Aided	Boys	50	- 0.0179	0.125	NS
		Girls	50	- 0.154	1.0922	NS
	Private	Boys	50	- 0.1006	0.733	NS
		Girls	50	- 0.1248	0.9242	NS

N.S – Not Significant

From the table 12, and also from figure M, In the case of boys and girls of Government, Government aided and Private school, the calculated coefficient values were less than that table of correlation coefficient values. Hence the hypothesis is accepted and proved that there are no significant relationship between Academic achievement and Shame of the sample.

Hypothesis -7

Education of father does not associate with Guilt of the total sample.

TABLE. 4.13: Chi- Square test between Father's Educational Qualifications with Guilt of the total sample.

Variable	Type of management	Gender	N	df	X^2	L.S
Father's Educational Qualification with Guilt	Government	Boys	50	4	1.8697	NS
		Girls	50	4	3.5434	NS
	Government Aided	Boys	50	4	1.0771	NS
		Girls	50	4	0.1944	NS
	Private	Boys	50	4	15.4984	0.01
		Girls	50	4	4.6484	NS

From the table 13, it is understood that calculated Chi-Square value is more than that of table values ($p<0.01$, N=50) in private boys. Hence the hypothesis is rejected and proved that there is significant association between Father's Educational Qualification with Guilt in the case of boys of private school.

In the case of boys and girls government and Government Aided and girls of private School the hypothesis is accepted since the calculated Chi-Square values were less than that of table values. Hence the hypothesis is accepted and proved that there are no significant associations between Father's Educational Qualification with Guilt in the above mentioned cases.

Hypothesis -8

Education of Mother does not associate with Guilt of the total sample.

TABLE .4.14: Chi – Square test between Mother Educational Qualification with Guilt of the total sample

Variable	Type of management	Gender	N	df	X^2	L.S
Mother's Educational Qualification with Guilt	Government	Boys	50	4	0.4361	NS
		Girls	50	4	7.4654	NS
	Government Aided	Boys	50	4	0.5995	NS
		Girls	50	4	0.5209	NS
	Private	Boys	50	4	2.8636	NS
		Girls	50	4	4.0816	NS

From the table 14, it is understood that calculated Chi-Square values is less than that of table values. Hence the hypothesis is accepted and proved that there are no significant association between Education of Mother with Guilt of boys and girls from the total sample.

Hypothesis -9

Occupation of father does not associate with Guilt of the total sample.

TABLE. 4.15: Chi-Square tests between Father Occupation with Guilt of the total sample.

Variable	Type of management	Gender	N	df	X^2	L.S
Father Occupation with Guilt	Government	Boys	50	4	1.0793	NS
		Girls	50	4	1.6901	0.05
	Government Aided	Boys	50	4	1.6578	NS
		Girls	50	4	1.409	NS
	Private	Boys	50	4	2.5	NS
		Girls	50	4	0.1661	NS

N.S – Not Significant

From the table 15, it is understood that calculated Chi-Square value is more than that of table values ($p<0.05$, $N=50$) in Government girls. Hence the hypothesis is rejected and proved that there is significant association between Father Occupation with Guilt in the case of girls' government school of sample.

In the case of boys Government School, boys and girls Government Aided and private School the hypothesis is accepted since the calculated Chi-Square values was less than that of table values. Hence the hypothesis is accepted and proved that there are no significant associations between Father Occupation with Guilt in the above mentioned cases.

Hypothesis -10

Occupation of Mother does not associate with Guilt of the total sample.

TABLE.4.16: Chi-Square tests between Mother Occupation with Guilt of the total sample.

Variable	Type of management	Gender	N	df	X^2	L.S
Mother Occupation with Guilt	Government	Boys	50	4	2.5888	NS
		Girls	50	4	2.254	NS
	Government Aided	Boys	50	4	3.6478	NS
		Girls	50	4	7.1513	NS
	Private	Boys	50	4	1.4408	NS
		Girls	50	4	0.1661	NS

N.S – Not Significant

From the table 16, it is understood that calculated Chi-Square values is less than that of table values. Hence the hypothesis is accepted and proved that there are no significant association between Occupation of Mother with Guilt of boys and girls from the total sample.

Hypothesis-11

Type of family does not associate with Guilt of the total sample.

TABLE. 4.17: Chi-Square test between types of family with Guilt of the total sample.

Variable	Type of management	Gender	N	df	X^2	L.S
Type of family with Guilt	Government	Boys	50	2	0.5209	NS
		Girls	50	2	1.1179	NS
	Government Aided	Boys	50	2	10.9012	0.05
		Girls	50	2	0.1661	NS
	Private	Boys	50	2	4.2112	NS
		Girls	50	2	2.2145	NS

N.S – Not Significant

From the table 17, it is understood that calculated Chi-Square value is more than that of table values ($p<0.05$, $N=50$) in Government aided boys. Hence the hypothesis is rejected and proved that there is significant association between Types of family with Guilt in the case of boy's government aided school of sample.

In the case of boys and girls Government School, girls of Government Aided School, boys and girls of private School the hypothesis is accepted since the calculated Chi-Square values were less than that of table values. Hence the hypothesis is accepted and proved that there are no significant associations between Types of family with Guilt in the above mentioned cases.

Hypothesis -12

Annual Income does not associate with Guilt of the total sample.

TABLE. 4.18: Chi-Square test between Annual Income with Guilt of the total sample.

Variable	Type of management	Gender	N	df	X^2	L.S
Annual Income with Guilt	Government	Boys	50	2	0.9735	NS
		Girls	50	2	4.9691	NS
	Government Aided	Boys	50	2	0.5876	NS
		Girls	50	2	0.1812	NS
	Private	Boys	50	2	0.8311	NS
		Girls	50	2	0.2892	NS

From the table 18, it is understood that calculated Chi-Square values is less than that of table values. Hence the hypothesis is accepted and proved that there are no significant association between Annual Income with Guilt of boys and girls from the total sample

Hypothesis -13

Educational of Father does not associate with Shame of the total sample.

TABLE4.19: Chi- Square tests between Father's Educational Qualification with Shame of the total sample.

Variable	Type of management	Gender	N	df	X^2	L.S
Father's Educational Qualification with Shame	Government	Boys	50	4	7.875	NS
		Girls	50	4	6.7387	NS
	Government Aided	Boys	50	4	2.3884	NS
		Girls	50	4	0.1943	NS
	Private	Boys	50	4	5.357	NS
		Girls	50	4	8.5931	NS

N.S – Not Significant

From the table 19, it is understood that calculated Chi-Square values is less than that of table values. Hence the hypothesis is accepted and proved that there are no significant association between Father's Educational Qualification and Shame of boys and girls from the total sample.

Hypothesis -14

Educational of Mother does not associate with Shame of the total sample.

TABLE. 4.20: Chi-Square tests between Mother's Educational Qualification with Shame of the total sample.

Variable	Type of management	Gender	N	df	X^2	L.S
Mother's Educational Qualification with Shame.	Government	Boys	50	4	2.0491	NS
		Girls	50	4	2.8846	NS
	Government Aided	Boys	50	4	1.0771	NS
		Girls	50	4	0.2247	NS
	Private	Boys	50	4	5.357	NS
		Girls	50	4	6.5943	NS

From the table 20, it is understood that calculated Chi-Square values is less than that of table values. Hence the hypothesis is accepted and proved that there are no significant association between Mother's Educational Qualification with Shame of boys and girls from the total sample.

Hypothesis -15

Occupations of Father do not associate with Shame of the total sample.

TABLE.4.21: Chi-Square tests between Father's Occupations with Shame of the total sample.

Variable	Type of management	Gender	N	df	X^2	L.S
Father Occupation with Shame	Government	Boys	50	4	0.7083	NS
		Girls	50	4	2.6147	NS
	Government Aided	Boys	50	4	5.1057	NS
		Girls	50	4	1.409	NS
	Private	Boys	50	4	0.7575	NS
		Girls	50	4	2.7721	NS

N.S – Not Significant

From the table 21, it is understood that calculated Chi-Square values is less than that of table values. Hence the hypothesis is accepted and proved that there are no significant association between Father's Occupations with Shame of boys and girls from the total sample.

Hypothesis -16

Occupations of Mother do not associate with Shame of the total sample.

TABLE. 4.22: Chi-Square tests between Mother's Occupations with Shame of the total sample.

Variable	Type of management	Gender	N	df	X^2	L.S
Mother Occupation with Shame	Government	Boys	50	4	1.3251	NS
		Girls	50	4	2.4872	NS
	Government Aided	Boys	50	4	1.2599	NS
		Girls	50	4	16.0137	0.01
	Private	Boys	50	4	5.4079	NS
		Girls	50	4	7.7635	NS

N.S – Not Significant

From the table 22, it is understood that calculated Chi-Square value is more than that of table values ($p<0.01$, N=50) in Government aided girls. Hence the hypothesis is rejected and proved that there is significant association between Mother Occupation with Shame.

In the case of girls of government aided school of the sample. In the case of boys and girls Government School, boys of Government Aided School, boys and girls private School the hypothesis is accepted since the calculated Chi-Square values was less than that of table values. Hence the hypothesis is accepted and proved that there are no significant associations between Mother Occupation with Shame. In the above mentioned cases.

Hypothesis -17

Types of family do not associate with Shame of the total sample.

TABLE .4.23: Chi-Square Tests between Types of family with Shame of the total sample.

Variable	Type of management	Gender	N	df	X^2	L.S
Type of family with Shame	Government	Boys	50	2	0.3995	NS
		Girls	50	2	3.2085	NS
	Government Aided	Boys	50	2	6.6393	0.05
		Girls	50	2	0.4233	NS
	Private	Boys	50	2	1.2914	NS
		Girls	50	2	0.574	NS

N.S – Not Significant

From the table 23, it is understood that calculated Chi-Square value is more than that of table values ($p<0.05$, N=50) in Government aided boys. Hence the hypothesis is rejected and proved that there is significant association between Types of family with Shame in the case of boys of Government aided school sample.

In the case of boys and girls Government school, girls of Government Aided School and boys and girls of private school the hypothesis is accepted since the calculated Chi-Square values were less than that of table values. Hence the hypothesis is accepted and proved that there are no significant associations between Types of family with Shame in the above mentioned cases.

Hypothesis -18

Annual Income does not associate with Shame of the total sample.

TABLE . 4.24: Chi-Square test between Annual Income with Shame of the total sample.

Variable	Type of management	Gender	N	df	X^2	L.S
Annual Income with Shame	Government	Boys	50	2	0.5928	NS
		Girls	50	2	1.6901	NS
	Government Aided	Boys	50	2	0.3968	NS
		Girls	50	2	0.0886	NS
	Private	Boys	50	2	40.5865	0.01
		Girls	50	2	0.6907	NS

N.S – Not Significant

From the table 24, it is understood that calculated Chi-Square value is more than that of table values ($p<0.01$, N=50) in private boys. Hence the hypothesis is rejected and proved that there is significant associations between Annual Income with Shame in the case of boys of private school sample.

In the case of boys and girls for Government and Government Aided School and girls of private school the hypothesis is accepted since the calculated Chi-Square values were less than that of table values. Hence the hypothesis is accepted and proved that there are no significant associations between Annual Income with Shame in the above mentioned cases.

CONCLUSION

This chapter explains the analysis of data, testing of hypotheses and interpretation of the data. A brief report of the research study together with the major findings, educational implications and the suggestions for further research has been discussed in succeeding chapter.

❐

5

Summary and Findings

This chapter provides a brief summary of the entire study gives interpretation of results obtained from the statistical analysis of the data presented in the previous chapter; also highlight the main findings of the study, points of the implication and recommendation for future study.

STATEMENT OF THE PROBLEM

"Guilt and Shame on Academic Achievement among higher secondary school" is the chosen for the study.

HYPOTHESES AND FINDING

1. **There are no significant differences between Guilt of Boys and Girls from the total sample**
   Hypothesis is accepted and proved that there are no significant differences between guilt of boys and girls from the Government and Government Aided School Hypothesis is rejected and proved that there are significant differences between guilt of boys and girls from the Private school
2. **There are no significant differences between Shame of boys and girls from the total sample**
   Hypothesis is accepted and proved that there is no significant differences between Shame of boys and girls from the Government and Government Aided School

Hypothesis is rejected and proved that there is significant differences between Shame of boys and girls from the Private School

3. **There are no significant differences between academic achievement of boys and girls from the total sample**
   Hypothesis is rejected and proved that there is significant differences between academic achievement of boys and girls from the Government School Hypothesis is accepted and proved that there are no significant differences between academic achievement of boys and girls from the Government Aided and Private School.
4. **There is no significant relationship between Guilt and Shame**
   Hypothesis is rejected proved that there is significant relationship between Guilt and Shame in the case of boys of government aided school Hypothesis is accepted and proved that there is no significant relationship between Guilt and Shame in the case of boys and girls Government school, girls Government Aided School and boys and girls of Private school
5. **There is no significant relationship between Guilt and Academic Achievement**
   Hypothesis is rejected and proved that there is significant relationship between Guilt and Academic Achievement in the case of boys of Government and girls of Private school
   Hypothesis is accepted and proved that there is no significant relationship between Guilt and Academic Achievement in the case of girls of Government school, boys and girls of Government Aided School and boys of Private school
6. **There is no significant relationship between academic achievement and Shame**
   Hypothesis is accepted and proved that there are no significant relationship between academic achievement and Shame of the total sample
7. **Education of father does not associate with Guilt**
   Hypothesis is rejected and proved that there is significant association between education of father and guilt in boys of private school from the total sample
   Hypothesis is accepted and proved that there is no significant association between education of father and guilt in girls of Private school and boys and girls of Government and Government Aided School
8. **Education of mother does not associate with Guilt**
   Hypothesis is accepted and proved that there are no significant association between education of mother and Guilt of boys and girls from the total sample.

9. **Occupation of father does not associate with Guilt**
Hypothesis is rejected and proved that there is significant association between occupation of father and guilt of girls of government school
Hypothesis is accepted and proved that there are no significant association between occupation of father and Guilt of boys of Government, boys and girls of Government Aided and Private school.

10. **Occupation of mother does not associate with Guilt**
Hypothesis is accepted and proved that there are no significant associations between occupation of mother and Guilt of boys and girls from the total sample.

11. **Type of family does not associate with Guilt**
Hypothesis is rejected and proved that there is significant association between Type of family and Guilt in the case of boys of Government Aided School
Hypothesis is accepted and proved that there are no significant association between Type of family and Guilt of girls of Government Aided, boys and girls of Government and Private school

12. **Annual income does not associate with Guilt**
Hypothesis is accepted and proved that there are no significant association between annual income and Guilt of boys and girls from the total sample.

13. **Education of father does not associate with Shame**
Hypothesis is accepted and proved that there are no significant association between Education of father and Shame of boys and girls from the total sample.

14. **Education of mother does not associate with Shame**
Hypothesis is accepted and proved that there are no significant association between Education of mother and Shame of boys and girls from the total sample.

15. **Occupation of father does not associate with Shame:-**
Hypothesis is accepted and proved that there are no significant association between Occupation of father and Shame of boys and girls from the total sample.

16. **Occupation of mother does not associate with Shame.**
The hypothesis is rejected and proved that there is significant association between occupation of mother and shame in the case of girls of government aided school.
Hypothesis is accepted and proved that there are no significant association between Occupation of mother and Shame in the case of boys of Government Aided School and boys and girls Government and Private school

17. Type of family do not associate with Shame

Hypothesis is rejected and proved that there is significant relationship between Type of family and Shame in the case of boys of Government Aided School

Hypothesis is accepted and proved that there are no significant association between Type of family and Shame in the case of girls of Government Aided School and boys and girls Government and Private school

18. Annual income does not associate with Shame.

Hypothesis is rejected and proved that there is significant association between Annual income and shame in the case of boys of private school

Hypothesis is accepted and proved that there are no significant association between Annual income and Shame in the case of girls of Private School and boys and girls Government and Government Aided School

Educational implications of the study

In India the quality improvement in education is the greatest need of the day. The quality education can be measured through academic achievement of the students. To achieve this goal positive attitude towards education should be inculcated in children. So that there may be higher motivation to develop their innate skills and become useful citizens of India.

Though the present study highlights there is no significant difference between boys and girls in their academic achievement, but students belonging to difference types of schools differ among themselves in their academic achievement. Hence, the educators and school management should take some effort to bring all round development of the students for better achievement under any circumstances.

Mind plays a flexible role in accomplishing variety of tasks. It is therefore important for the parents and the teachers to understand the nature of the student's mind and its functions in different styles of learning and thinking.

Teachers can only make a child to mould the behaviour dominance according to the different types of activities dominance.

❐

6

The Problem and its Perspectives

Education is very important for an individual's success in life. Education provides pupils teaching skills that prepare them physically, mentally and socially for the world in later life. Education is generally seen as the foundation of society which brings economic wealth, social prosperity and political stability. Education is major aspect of development of any modern society since if there is a deficit of educated people then society will stops its further progress. Government should pay serious attention to education and support it economically and morally all over the country.

Education by its emphases practices the slaying of Sir William Hamilton, "In the world there is nothing great but man; in man there is nothing great but mind". Education shows us a development, the unrealized powers of mind through exercise becoming actualized. Education is the process of evolution which becomes conscious of itself. As a significant conscious process of development in time, whereby immaturity reaches maturity and the child becomes a man, education ought to be a chapter in the serial which universe is writing through time in the heavens and upon the earth.

COOPERATIVE LEARNING

Cooperative learning is a student-centred, instructor-facilitated instructional strategy in which a small group of students is responsible for its own learning and the learning of all group members. Students interact with each other in the same group to acquire and practice the elements of a subject matter in order to solve a problem, complete a task or achieve a goal.

Cooperative learning is an instructional strategy that uses small groups of students working together and helping one another on specific learning tasks with an emphasis on group members supporting one another.

Cooperative Learning is a very formal way of structuring activities in a learning environment that includes specific elements intended to increase the potential for rich and deep learning by the students.

This type of learning has been called by various names: cooperative learning, collaborative learning, collective learning, learning communities, peer teaching, peer learning, or team learning. Collaboration entails the whole process of learning. This may include students teaching one another, students teaching the teacher, and of course the teacher teaching the students, too. More importantly, it means that students are responsible for one another's learning as well as their own and that reaching the goal implies that students have helped each other to understand and learn.

Collaborative learning, on the other hand, is aimed at getting the students to take almost full responsibility for working together, building knowledge together, changing and evolving together and of course, improving together.

DEFINITION OF COOPERATIVE LEARNING

According to Johnson et al (1998) is the "instructional use of small groups so that students' work together to maximise their own and each other's learning."

According to Gillies, R., (2007) Cooperative learning involves students working together in small groups to accomplish shared goals.

According to Slavin (1980), "the term refers to classroom techniques in which students work on learning activities in small groups and receive rewards or recognition based on their group's performance".

BASIC PRINCIPLES OF COOPERATIVE LEARNING

- Positive interdependence is built in – cooperation is necessary for students to succeed.
- Attention and class time are given to interpersonal/cooperative skill building.
- Students learn together in small (2-5 members) groups.
- Students are individually accountable for learning and participation.
- The instructor's role changes from being the "sage on the stage" to the "guide on the side."

Cooperative Learning is about moving from rote learning to learning how to think critically and in changing circumstances.

The consistent use of these principles in an organized way is at the heart of Cooperative Learning.

BASIC ELEMENTS OF COOPERATIVE LEARNING

David W. Johnson, Roger T. Johnson, Edythe, J. Holubec and others identify five basic elements of cooperative learning.

- Positive Interdependence
- Individual Accountability
- Group Processing
- Skilled Interpersonal Communication
- Face-to-Face Primitive Interactions

Positive Interdependence

Team members are obliged to rely on one another to achieve the goal. If any team members fail to do their part, everyone suffers consequences.

Interaction through Activity

Learners help, assist, encourage, and support each others' efforts to learn.

Individual Accountability

The performance of each individual learner is assessed and the results given back to the group and the individual.

All students in a group are held accountable for doing their share of the work and for mastery of all of the material to be learned.

Group Processing

Team members set group goals, periodically assess what they are doing well as a team, and identify changes they will make to function more effectively in the future.

Cooperative learning is not simply a synonym for students working in groups.

Interaction through Reflection

At the end of their working period the groups process their functioning by answering two questions:

1. What did each member do that was helpful for the group? And
2. What can each member do to make the group work better?

Skilled Interpersonal Communication

Skilled communication is necessary for effective group functioning. Learners must have, and use, the needed leadership, decision making, trust-building, effective communication, and conflict-management skills.

Appropriate use of collaborative skills

Students are encouraged and helped to develop and practice trust-building, leadership, decision-making, communication, and conflict management skills.

Face-to-Face Primitive Interactions

Although some of the group work may be parcelled out and done individually, some must be done interactively, with group members providing one another with feedback, challenging reasoning and conclusions, and perhaps most importantly, teaching and encouraging one another.

Interdependence through Structure

Learners believe that they are linked together; they cannot succeed unless the other members of the group succeed (and vice versa). They "sink or swim together."

Other Elements of Cooperative Learning

Spencer Kagen in Cooperative Learning, Resources for Teachers (1994) identify the needed elements as: Positive Interdependence, Individual Accountability, Equal Participation, and Simultaneous Interaction.

THE QUALITY OF COOPERATIVE LEARNING

Cooperative learning is not just a learning theory or a teaching method, it refers to a set of instructional principles that together describe how students might learn from and with each other and, through working together, accomplish academic tasks.

Successful cooperative learning situations require in the first place that students have positive beliefs about cooperative learning. In order to feel responsible for group learning students also need to be aware of the skills that should be used and have easy access to these skills.

REASONS TO USE COOPERATIVE LEARNING

1. Adults often manage conflicts destructively. Everyone tend to behave as they have been taught. A highly individualistic and competitive environment may lead to an inability to get along or manage conflicts constructively.
2. Industry requires people who can work cooperatively in teams. The Conference Board of Canada has said that learners need academic

skills, personal skills and cooperative or teamwork skills. Schools and colleges generally do a good job of the academic skills but often neglect the personal and teamwork skills because they see them as the responsibility of the home. With family life changing, many learners do not develop these skills at home.

3. Researchers have found that 90 to 95% of the people who lose their jobs do so because they cannot get along with other people on the job. Only 5 or 10 percent (depending on which studies you read) of people lose their jobs because they cannot do the work. Cooperative learning helps people learn social skills and therefore increases the chances that they will be able to keep the jobs for which we are training them.
4. In schools, learners bring with them their own negative attitudes and prejudices. Population diversity is becoming more the norm than the exception in many places. When there is a mix of learners in the same class there is the potential to diminish negative attitudes and to develop positive ones depending how interaction is structured. Cooperative learning structures can be used to develop constructive and supportive peer relationships.

TYPES OF COOPERATIVE LEARNING GROUPS

There are three basic types of cooperative learning groups

- Base or Home groups
- Formal cooperative learning groups
- Informal cooperative learning groups.

Base or Home Groups

Base groups are long-term cooperative learning groups with stable membership. Learners are chosen for base groups in a manner that will guarantee a good mix of academic levels in the group. These groups are set up to so that members provide support to each other so that all can succeed academically.

For example, students may work or take notes for each other if one of the group members is absent, and they will coach each other to prepare for individual tests.

The use of base groups tends to personalize the classroom, improve attendance and also improve the quality and quantity of learning. Teachers should use base group for higher learning.

The more learners you have in a class and the more complex the subject matter, the more important it is to have base groups organized. The members should be compatible and supportive.

Formal Cooperative Learning Groups

These groups may last from several minutes to several class sessions to complete a specific task or assignment (such as doing a set of problems, completing a unit of work, writing a report, conducting an experiment, or reading and comprehending a story, play, chapter or book). The members are carefully chosen for heterogeneity to maximize learning and minimize 'group think'.

For example, students who join during any practical work and group assignment and leave each other after the particular event completed mostly they are framed by the instructions of the class teacher.

Informal Cooperative Learning Groups

These groups are temporary, ad hoc groups that last for a few minutes, one discussion or class period. The members are often chosen randomly and will rotate on a regular basis. Their purposes are to focus learner attention on the material to be learned, create an expectation set and mood conducive to learning, as well as help organize in advance the material to be covered in a class session. They can ensure that learners cognitively process the material being taught and provide closure to an instructional session. They may be used at any time but they are especially useful during a lecture or direct reading. The length of time that most college learners can attend to a lecture before they begin to drift away is around 20 to 25 minutes. These groups help break up the lecture and allow learners to process the content as they take part in class.

COOPERATIVE LEARNING CHARACTERIZED THROUGH THE FOLLOWING ACTIVITIES

1. Require students to depend on one another for success. Having student's sit side by side working on something they could just as easily do by themselves in not cooperative learning. Students must be required to share materials, knowledge, time, talents, and effort (or any combination of these).
2. Provide for individual accountability. Group members share jobs and make group presentations. Group members are tested individually and/or as a group to ensure that each person has mastered the required learning.
3. Utilizes face-to-face interaction among students. For all group work students are arranged in close proximity of each other. They can be at tables, in desks or chairs pushed together, on the floor, or virtually anywhere they can do the task at hand separated from other groups.

4. Focus on interpersonal and group skills. Tasks are designed to include components of positive interpersonal communication skills such as active listening, building consensus, sharing, supporting, restating, using appropriate eye contact and gestures, and encouraging. Teams learn to stay on task and check each other for understanding.

EFFECTIVE USE OF COOPERATIVE LEARNING

- Increase achievement (at all ability levels)
- Empower students to take responsibility for their own learning
- Improve retention
- Generate more positive feelings towards the subject matter
- Provide more active learning
- Focus more time on learning
- Lower frustration and anxiety among students
- Enhance a sense of community among students
- Promote inter-personal communication skills
- Boost feelings of self-worth

ALTERNATIVE WAYS TO USE COOPERATIVE LEARNING

There are few ways to use cooperative learning as alternative they are a lecture or presentation, higher level questioning, practice reinforcement, Decision-making/problem solving, a review, tournament or game format, peer editing, assessment, Research projects or group investigations, Checking homework.

IMPLEMENTING COOPERATIVE LEARNING

The benefits of using cooperative learning are well supported by theory and well established by classroom research, but the method is not without its problems, most of which have to do with individual student resistance and dysfunctional teams. Many techniques have been developed that minimize the problems, most of which involve addressing one or more of the five criteria for cooperative learning. Rather, instructors new to cooperative learning should take a more gradual approach, choosing mainly the methods with which they feel most comfortable and adopting additional methods only when they have had time to get used to the current ones.

CO-OPERATIVE LEARNING METHODS

There are many quite different forms of co-operative learning, but all of them involve having students work in small groups or teams to help one another learn academic material. Co-operative learning usually supplements the teacher's instruction by giving students an opportunity to discuss information or practise skills originally presented by the teacher. Sometimes co-operative methods require students to find or discover information on their own. Co-operative learning has been used and investigated in every subject at all grade levels.

COOPERATIVE LEARNING METHODS - MAIN CATEGORIES

There are two main categories in cooperative learning methods

a. STRUCTURED TEAM LEARNING METHODS

This methods - involves rewards to teams based on the learning progress of their members, and they are also characterised by individual accountability, which means that team success depends on individual learning, not group products.

- Student Team Learning
- Student Teams-Achievement Divisions (STAD)
- Teams-Games-Tournament (TGT)
- Team Assisted Individualisation (TAI)
- Co-operative Integrated Reading and Composition (CIRC)
- Peer-Assisted Learning Strategies (PALS)

b. INFORMAL GROUP LEARNING METHODS

This method covers methods more focused on social dynamics, projects, and discussion than on mastery of well-specified content.

- Jigsaw
- Learning Together
- Group Investigation

COOPERATIVE LEARNING GROUPS

Group sizes

The ideal size for cooperative learning groups according to most experts in the field is four learners per group. When you have four in a group, you can have pairs working together at times and four working together at other times. There are six different pair combinations possible in groups of four.

There are many ways an instructor can place learners into groups. The following are a few ways this can be done:

1. Instructor Assigned Groups

The instructor can assign learners to groups to ensure that the groups are heterogeneous. The real advantage to forming groups in this manner is that instructors can see to it that groups are heterogeneous in terms of academic ability, ethnic background, gender, and any other factors that they feel are important.

The instructor tries to make sure that best friends and worst enemies are not in the same groups. If they are, communication patterns in the group are not as effective.

The most effective groups are usually the instructor assigned groups because they are more likely to be heterogeneous. Random groups and the others are very useful for short-term assignments, projects, but should not be used all the time or learners miss out on a lot of the advantages of working with heterogeneous groups.

2. Randomly Assigned Groups

The instructor can simply have learners number off, placing all the ones in one group, etc.

3. Social Integration Groups

The instructor can ask learners to privately name learners they would like to work with and any they would not like to work with in groups, and use this information to construct groups.

4. Subject-Matter Related Groups

If a group of learners are interested in a particular topic, they could be assigned to the same group to research and present the topic to the rest of the class.

5. Geographic Groups

Particularly useful for formal or base groups, this allows participants who live near each other to have a greater ease in meeting.

6. Self-Selected Groups

The instructor can simply ask learners to form their own groups – "Find three other people to work with on this project." This can work well for short-term groups but can be counterproductive if participants always end up in the same groupings.

These elements, learning groups and various learning methods of cooperative work have been discussed clearly in this research in different headings. This cooperative learning is expressed along with the achievement in Chemistry for clear understanding.

ADVANTAGES OF USING COOPERATIVE LEARNING

Cooperative learning is supported by one of the strongest research traditions in education, with thousands of studies conducted across a wide range of subject areas, age groups, ability levels and cultural backgrounds.

The result, in general, suggest that cooperative learning develops high-order thinking skills, enhances motivation and improve interpersonal relations as well as enhancing motivation and peer relations (Slavin, 1985).

Students can be learning-independent, who can learn how to learn by their own in groups. This is crucial as 'learning how to learn' is what being emphasized in the education reform in Hong Kong.

Most important is that cooperative learning exploits the diversified abilities of students to increase their cognitive, psychological and social performance, and as such, it is an effective way to address the problem of individual differences.

MEANING OF ACHIEVEMENT

As Baker says "The occurrence of success and failure experience is independent of actual achievement, it is determined, rather by the goals, expectations and aspirations of the person at the time of the action".

Achievement is actual performance. It is what a person does, regardless of his capacities. Achievement can never rally exceed aptitude though sometimes it may appear to do so.

THE CONCEPT OF ACHIEVEMENT

Achievement in actual performance; It is what a student does, regardless of his capacities. Achievement can never really exceed aptitude though sometimes, it may appear to do so.

Achievement in the higher secondary level of one's academic career is the most important goal in one's life. This necessitates their improvement in study and acquisition of higher scores in all subjects they have chosen for study.

DEFINITIONS OF THE ACHIEVEMENT

According to Henry E. Garrett, "Achievement means actual performance, often used in reference to scores on educational tests or to schools grades".

According to Good (1945), academic achievement is the knowledge attained or skills developed in the school subjects usually assessed by test scores or by marks assigned by teachers or by both.

According to Lidgrem (1965) "Schools and colleges are geared to the marks getting racket and it in a situation that is going to continue to be the only criteria for qualifying for the next step in the onward and upward journey to better things".

Accomplishment or proficiency of performance in a given skill or body knowledge; (ii) Progress in school, theoretically different from intelligence but overlaps with it to a great degree (Good, 1973).

Refers to performance in school or college in a standardized series of educational test (Taneja, 1991).

Accomplishment of specified objectives, (ii) past performance, (iii) what an individual or organization has accomplished in the past in contrast with 'ability' which refers to what an individual or organization can do now (in the present) or in the future (Madhu Raj, 1996).

Successful accomplishment or performance in particular subjects, areas, courses, usually by reasons of skill, hard work and interest. Typically summarized in various types of grades, marks, scores or descriptive commentary (John Bellingham, 2004)

LEVEL OF ACHIEVEMENT

Bloom analysis suggests the important of the pre-school period and the first few years of school life on the development of learning patterns and general achievement. The two differences of scholastic achievement according to him are as follows:

1. The meaning which education comes to have for the child in respect of his own personal advancement and role in society.
2. Also the level of education and value placed on education by parents and other significant adults in the child's life and the extent to which scholastic achievement is motivated and reinforced by these adults.

ACADEMIC ACHIEVEMENT

The meaning of the term "achievement" must be considered in relation to student's involvement in schools. It is important to know how the achievement was measured before conclusions can be drawn about the relationship between students and academic achievement. More often than not standardized test scores are used to determine how well students are doing in school standardized testing is taken for granted in this country.

In relief, these tests are determinants of accountability a term used by those in power that need to know how effectively systems work. In recent years, testing programs have increased (Kamil 1990) raising scores and having a good appearance are the goals for most schools because newspapers and other media rank schools and districts by test scores other facts of society also rely on these test scores to determine the "best" schools. Waragh and Comuntziz-page (1996) have pointed out the inadequacies of mixing a more holistic curriculum with traditional pencil looking beyond the traditional evaluation methods.

Gardner (1993) also agrees that academic achievement should be measured in a number of ways, According to him. "Assessment, then becomes a central feature of an Educational system, we believe that it is essential to depart from standardized testing, we also believe pencil and paper short-answer tests sample only a small proportion of intellectual facility. The means of assessment we favour should ultimately search for genuine problem – solving or product fashioning skills in individuals across a range at materials.

SIGNIFICANCE OF ACADEMIC ACHIEVEMENT

The perplexing phenomena of academic under achievement and failures among students at various stages of education have been and continue to be a cause of grave concern to the Educationalists, teachers, guidance counsellors and Educational planners. In the world over for those in developing countries like India, in particular due to heavy investment in education. This is a grave concern Radha K. Sharma (1985) academic achievement at secondary level is of crucial importance to,

1. Students as their future career are decided on the basis of their education.
2. Higher secondary institution as it affects their reputation and
3. Educationalist as a higher secondary stage us a link between school and higher education. Low achievement and failure cause lack of self-confidence is students which make them sceptical of their abilities and causing inferiority complex in them.

FACTORS AFFECTING ACADEMIC ACHIEVEMENT OF STUDENTS

The factors which affect the Academic Achievement of the children includes the class marks, time spent in going and returning from school, parental interest in education of pupils, family size, leisure time activities facilities in the school, home work, and class tests. Attitudes towards school life, type of punishment in the school, attendance, co-curricular activities and involvement in sports build up the student's personality. The factors that affect the academic achievement of the students can be classified into three major headings.

1. Teacher Factor
2. Social and educational factors
3. Organizational and administrative factors.

1. Teacher Factor

Teachers are very important in giving the right academic guidance and input on a day to day basis which surely affects the academic achievement of the students. It is also seen that good competent teachers have a direct input on the academic achievement of students.

2. Social and Educational Factors

The social set up where the child comes from also has a definite impact on the academic achievement of students. The home environment and the neighbourhood from where he hails provides the security support, encouragement that if needed to achieve high in life.

3. Organizational and Administrative Factors

Students who generally achieve well in academics are moulded by the good facilities that are provided by the educational institutions. The organizational climate existing within the schools indirectly supports in reacting for the academic goals the student has set. The administrative heads act as a backbone to lift up the students who require that extra effort and encourage them from behind the screen for the academic achievement in the end examinations.

ACHIEVEMENT IN CHEMISTRY

For this study researcher chosen to focus on student preparation and performance in the area of Chemistry. Chemistry is commonly viewed as the "central science" as mastery of its concepts regarding the structure of matter is essential to further course work in all science. Chemistry performs the function of gatekeeper for future study in many sciences. Thus it would appear that population for Chemistry at school level would be an important consideration and in most cases.

IMPORTANCE OF CHEMISTRY SUBJECT

Science education can exert a dominant, if not decisive influence on the life of individual as well as on the developmental effort of a nation (Emovon, 1985). The universal recognition of the above submission is responsible for the prime position that has been accorded science and in particular, Chemistry worldwide. Within the context of science education, Chemistry has been identified as a very important school subject and its importance in scientific and technological development of any nation has been widely reported. It was as a result of the recognition given to Chemistry in the development of the individual and the nation. Its inclusion as a core subject in science in the secondary school calls for the need to teach it effectively.

This is because effective science teaching can lead to the attainment of scientific and technological greatness. Chemistry teaching can only be result-oriented when students are willing and the teachers are favourably disposed, suing the appropriate methods and resources in teaching the students. With the current increase in scientific knowledge the world over much demand is placed, and emphasis is laid on the teacher, the learner, the curriculum and the environment in the whole process of teaching and learning of science.

This study seeks to provide a bond between Cooperative learning and Achievement in Chemistry.

STATEMENT OF THE PROBLEM

The present study is entitled as, "A study on Cooperative learning and Achievement in Chemistry of higher secondary students in Vellore district.

OPERATIONAL DEFINITION

Cooperative Learning

According to the Johnson & Johnson model (2000) cooperative learning is instruction that involves students working in teams to accomplish a common goal.

This questionnaire is prepared by the investigator with the help of guide Mr. D. Arnold Robinson (2014) it is consist of three dimensions such as influence of peer group, interest, and teaching method. The score obtained from this questionnaire is considered as the cooperative learning of an individual.

Achievement in Chemistry

Achievement means actual performance often used in reference to score on Educational tests or to school grades. Here achievement in Chemistry refers to the marks obtained by the XI standard students to the special tool from Chemistry subject which is prepared by the investigator. The score obtained from this questionnaire is considered as the achievement in Chemistry of an individual.

Need for the Study

Education is very important to everyone to lead a successful life. The social and technical change has a great affect on student's academic progress. The problem of any institution and every teacher is to find out ways to improve the academic achievement of the students. The teachers are an important constituency in the in structural process that can plan very important role in providing good efforts to the students for their academic progress.

A good teacher can find out desirable and undesirable character and abilities in the students in order to motivate their individual efforts on academic achievement. Thereby their academic performance may be increased to through this study it was attempted to predict the favourable conditions. The present study aims to find out that influence of peer group, interest of student and various methodologies in teaching learning process are interrelated and a positive influence on academic achievement.

Cooperative learning is supported by one of the strongest research traditions in education, with many hundreds of studies conducted across a wide range of subject areas and age groups. This Research suggests that student to student collaboration conducted in a manner consistent with cooperative learning principles produces superior results on a host of achievement in Chemistry.

OBJECTIVES OF THE STUDY

1. To find out the level of cooperative learning of higher secondary school students.
2. To find out the level of achievement in Chemistry of higher secondary school students.
3. To find out the significant difference in Cooperative learning of higher secondary school students based on gender.
4. To find out the significant difference in achievement in Chemistry of higher secondary school students based on gender.
5. To find out the significant difference in Cooperative learning of higher secondary school students based on types of management.
6. To find out the significant difference in achievement in Chemistry of higher secondary school students based on types of management.
7. To find out the significant difference in Cooperative learning of higher secondary school students based on types of family.
8. To find out the significant difference in achievement in Chemistry of higher secondary school students based on types of family.
9. To find out the significant difference in Cooperative learning of higher secondary school students based on medium of learning.
10. To find out the significant difference in achievement in Chemistry of higher secondary school students based on medium of learning.
11. To find out the significant difference in Cooperative learning of higher secondary school students based on father's educational qualification.
12. To find out the significant difference in achievement in Chemistry of higher secondary school students based father's educational qualification.
13. To find out the significant difference in Cooperative learning of higher secondary school students based on father's occupation.
14. To find out the significant difference in achievement in Chemistry of higher secondary school students based on father's occupation.
15. To find out the significant difference in Cooperative learning of higher secondary school students based on mother's educational qualification.
16. To find out the significant difference in achievement in Chemistry of higher secondary school students based on mother's educational qualification.

17. To find out the significant difference in Cooperative learning of higher secondary school students based on mother's occupation.
18. To find out the significant difference in achievement in Chemistry of higher secondary school students based on mother's occupation.
19. To find out the significant difference in Cooperative learning of higher secondary school students based on the fields of Interest.
20. To find out the significant difference in achievement in Chemistry of higher secondary school students based on the fields of Interest.
21. To find out the significant difference in Cooperative learning of higher secondary school students based on locality of house.
22. To find out the significant difference in achievement in Chemistry of higher secondary school students based on locality of house.
23. To find out the significant difference in Cooperative learning of higher secondary school students based on the mode of transport.
24. To find out the significant difference in achievement in Chemistry of higher secondary school students based on the mode of transport.
25. To find out the significant difference in Cooperative learning of higher secondary school students based on family monthly income.
26. To find out the significant difference in achievement in Chemistry of higher secondary school students based on family monthly income.
27. To find out the significant difference in Cooperative learning of higher secondary school students based on their wake up time during school days.
28. To find out the significant difference in achievement in Chemistry of higher secondary school students based on their wake up time during school days.
29. To find out the significant difference in Cooperative learning of higher secondary school students based on their usage of mobile phones.
30. To find out the significant difference in achievement in Chemistry of higher secondary school students based on their usage of mobile phones.
31. To find out the significant difference in Cooperative learning of higher secondary school students based on learning through Tuition.
32. To find out the significant difference in achievement in Chemistry of higher secondary school students based on learning through Tuition.
33. To find out the significant relationship between cooperative learning and achievement in Chemistry of higher secondary school students.

DELIMITATION OF THE STUDY

Researcher has framed the following delimitation for her research.

- This study is restricted only to 320 students.
- The study is conducted in Vellore districts only.
- The study is restricted only for higher secondary students.

CONCLUSION

In the first chapter, a brief outline of the variable such as Cooperative learning and Achievement in Chemistry of higher secondary students is discussed. The researcher revisited the theory behind the variables, characteristics, methodology and definitions related to the study. Researchers have been collected various reviews and they are given in the following chapter. ❐

7

Review of Related Literature

In this chapter the related literature with regard to the various variables involved in the present study have been reviewed so as to get proper theoretical orientation of the problem in hand. Only after going through the relevant studies conducted in India as well as abroad regarding cooperative learning and achievement in Chemistry one will be in a better position to investigate the problem of framing good hypotheses, planning for suitable tools and techniques, collecting appropriate data and analyzing the data with good theoretical perspective.

For any worthwhile study in any field of knowledge, the research work needs adequate familiarity with the work which has already been done in the area of his choice. In review of related studies, the researcher attempts to determine what other has learned about similar research problems and together information relevant to the research problem. The review of related literature serves multiple purposes and is essential to a well-designed research study.

STUDIES ON COOPERATIVE LEARNING

Slavin (1991), conducted a research on cooperative learning strategies to improve the achievement of students and their interpersonal relationships. In 67 studies of the achievement effects of cooperative learning 61% found significantly greater achievement in cooperative than in traditionally taught control groups. Positive effects were found in all major subjects all grade levels, in urban, rural and suburban schools and for high, average, and low achievers.

Maheady, Mallette, Harper and Sacca (1991), compared the effects of numbered heads together to a whole group questioning strategy on social studies tests scores with third graders students always performed better when numbered heads together was used and on task rates were approximately twice as high using this structure. The purpose of this study is to investigate the effects of Kagan's cooperative learning structures as a teaching method to increase student achievement in social studies classes with sixth graders.

Kagan (1994), examined and found out through his research that grouping is essential to cooperative learning. The most widely used team formation is that of heterogeneous teams, containing a high, two middle, and a low achieving student and having a mix of gender and ethnic diversity that reflect the classroom population. The rationale for heterogeneous groups argues that this produces the greatest opportunities for peer tutoring and supports as well as improving cross-race and cross-sex relations and integration occasionally, random or special interest teams could be formed to maximize student talents or meet a specific student need.

Sapon - Shevin (1994), explained cooperative learning has been found to be a successful teaching strategy at all levels, from Pre-school to post secondary. The developmental characteristics of middle school students make cooperative learning a good fit of teaching strategy for the needs of the students. Young adolescents need to socialize, be a part of a group share feelings, receive emotional support, and learn to see things from other perspectives. Cooperative learning groups do not separate students on the basis of class, race or gender and the goals of middle schools are consistent with the goals of cooperative learning theories. It is a peer centred pedagogy that promotes academic achievement and builds positive social relationships.

Nath & Ross (1996), studied that teachers using Student Teams Achievement Divisions (STAD) found that if teachers did not strictly adhere to the frame work of cooperative learning. The method was unsuccessful and students spent more time on disagreements or conflict management than they did on academic tasks.

Sparapani, Abel, Easton, Edwards and Herbster (1997), specified that teachers are likely to use a combination of methods. This resulted in very few activities that involved higher level thinking skills and most of the observations were to drill and review or routine activities. The reason for lack of teacher training is given as lack of funding and administrative support.

Goodwin (1999), pointed out that the framework of cooperative learning groups, students learn how to interact with their peers and increase involvement with the school community. Positive interactions do not always occur naturally and social skills instruction must precede and concur with the cooperative learning strategies. Social skills encompass communicating, building and maintaining trust, providing leadership and managing conflicts.

Johnson, Johnson and Stanne (2000), summarize that cooperative learning strategies are widely used because they are based on theory validated by research and almost any teacher can find a way to use cooperative learning methods that are consistent with personal philosophies. In a meta-analysis of 158 studies, Johnson & Johnson report that current research findings present evidence that cooperative learning methods are likely to produce positive achievement results.

The studies included eight methods of cooperative learning: learning together and alone, constructive controversy. Jigsaw procedure Student Teams Achievement Divisions (STAD), Team Accelerated Instruction (TAI), Cooperative Integrated Reading and Composition (CIRC),Teams Games Tournaments (TGT), and Group investigation. No studies were found that specifically investigate Kagan's cooperative learning structures. In each case, the achievement levels were significantly higher when cooperative learning methods were used as compared to individualistic or competitive methods of learning.

Glenn.T et.al (2013), conducted a meta-analysis on the effectiveness of cooperative and collaborative learning to support enhanced literacy outcomes. Inversions considered were provided in regular education settings (i.e. not pull-out instruction) with students from grades 2 through 12. Reviewing more than 30 years of literacy research, we located 18 intervention studies with 29 study cohorts. Included studies primarily used standardized assessments to report on students reading, vocabulary, or comprehension achievement, which we analyzed separately.

Overall, a student has significantly higher literacy achievement scores when instructional interventions utilized cooperative and collaborative activity structures. The overall weighted mean effect sizes ranged from 0.16 to 0.22 ("p" < 0.01) with more than 94% of the point estimates being positive. Because cooperative or collaborative learning was always one of multiple intervention components, it was impossible to estimate the unique, added effects of cooperative learning. Although the small number of eligible studies precludes any claims about the effectiveness of specific forms of grouping and the circumstances under which programs have more impact, our findings suggest that cooperative learning group was a core component of effective literacy interventions, particularly at the elementary level.

Roger T. Smith et.al (2014), described cooperative learning is an example of how theory validated by research may be applied to instructional practice. The major theoretical base for cooperative learning is social interdependence theory. It provides clear definitions of cooperative competitive and individualistic learning. Hundreds of research studies have validated its basic propositions and demonstrated that cooperative learning (compared with competitive and individualistic learning) increases student's efforts to achieve, encourages positive relationships with classmates and faculty, and improves. Psychological health and well being operational procedures have been derived from the validated theory to implement cooperative learning in university classes, including those needed to implement formal cooperative learning, informal cooperative learning and cooperative base groups.

STUDIES ON ACHIEVEMENT IN CHEMISTRY

Joseph steve (1986), conducted a study with a purpose to determine, if science learning environment could be used to predict achievement in a commitment to science. The original data collected from a large school system in a North Carolina using 5000 students.

It was shown that achievement in science was strongly related to concurrent achievement in other subject. Science concept was a significant predictor of achievement of some level of science students. Students were grouped by differential levels of achievement in science versus achievement in other subject areas this process identified the students attitudes, were more powerful indicators of achievement in science.

Estrop David .C (1987), had tested the relative influence of size on school of academic achievement. Six hundred and seventeen students from XI grade in state of illionus U.S were analyzed. A basic relation between size of high school and academic achievement was found. Three intervening variables were found to contribute meaningfully to the noted relationship.

Sudhir and Muraledharan pillai (1987), administered a science achievement test, a group test of intelligence and Socio-Economic status scale to 146 male and 165 female students of Indian secondary schools. No gender difference in science achievement was found; but high Socio-Economic status and high I.Q students have higher science achievement scores than low Socio-Economic and low I.Q group.

Mahashbele R.S (1990), had tested the relative influence of principals and teachers efficiency on academic achievement of students and found no significant relation between them about 25 principals and 500 teachers from polytechnic colleges were involved in the study along with their students.

Shah B.B (1990), in his work submitted to University of Madras made a study on an experimental investigation of selected teaching of creative thinking and achievement in science. The research was conducted with VII standard students. There were significant difference between the four selected strategies in developing creative thinking and achievement in science at 0.01 levels.

Dennis. A (1991), conducted a study on rural school science teaching; what affects achievement. Reports a study to investigate the factors that affect science achievement in rural secondary schools data from multiple sources provided a profile of the science programs and teachers and factor analysis identified groupings related to science achievement that included teacher variables, student and teacher attendance and teacher in service education variables.

Malcom. J, Michael. G (1991), conducted the study of the science achievement of year 12 students in Australia, ACER Research Monograph No.40. This report sets our results for Australia arising from its participation in the Second International Science Study (SISS). The focus is on year 12 students, including those studying science and those not currently studying science. Most of the results for the science students are presented separately for those specializing in biology, Chemistry or physics. In addition to measures of science achievement, the report deals with the extent to which students remain at school until year 12, and pursue the study of science, and a range of factors associated with the learning of science. Finally, in the conclusion the report includes an overview of results for the other 16 countries with comparable results at the upper secondary level.

Robert. P (1991), conducted the study of declines in science achievement; implications for public education. A major difficulty in trying to improve the level of achievement in public schools in the United States is that there is little consensus on the nature of the causes or the solution to the current educational problems. The variety and range of proposed solutions have grown as the inability of schools to restore science achievement has become more evident. This research focuses on changes in four of the variables related to science achievement: teachers, students, curricula, and school grades.

Forbes Roy. H (1993), made a detailed study on 94 secondary schools from North Carolina funding effects on depth of the curriculum, based on course offered, school enrolment and staffing, school size and location, funding levels and students achievement in 8 selected subjects. It was found that funding helps in developing infrastructure like special equipments, building, laboratories etc. A regression analysis indicates that fund level was a predictor of students achievement in Algebra, Chemistry and geometry while school size was a predictor of achievement in Biology and Physics.

Kahn, Eileen Moley (1995), examined student achievement and curriculum delivery method for each of the eight science objectives measured by the TAAS (Texas Assessment of Academic Skills) exam. Ten school districts were selected from those throughout the state using science curriculum delivery mode, geographic location and demographic data for stratified random sampling. There was a total of 8,869 students involved in this study. For this study, five of the district used printed page text and five of the districts used laser disenchanted delivery. From this analysis in all group studies, there was no significant difference in achievement.

Williard. J and Rodney. L (1998), conducted the study of science achievement in the United States and sixteen countries a report to the public. The second international IEA science study (SISS) had participants from 24 countries. In this report the data collected in 17 countries are analyzed and reported. Students from the 5th, 9th and 12th grades were opinions, a science teaching and learning inventory tests were analyzed. In addition teachers were asked to indicate the extent to which their students had an opportunity to learn the concepts tested by each questions, and these opportunities to learn (OTL) results are given in this report.

Wallace, and Stephen. R (1998), clarified the muddled state of the magnitude and direction of the relationship among attitudes towards science and science achievement as students progressed from middle school into high school. Data collected from the longitudinal study of American youth (LSAY) over a three year period were used to create and test the structural equation model. Results of this study indicate enquiry based instruction is effective in positively influencing 7th and 8th grade students understanding of science concepts.

Taiwanese Representative sample study (2007), reveals the interrelationship between senior high school students and their self-confidence and interest in science approximately 1,044, eleventh grade students from 30 classes attending four high schools throughout Taiwan was the sample of study. Statistical evidences proved that there exist a relationship between student's achievement and self confidence for a moderate effect science.

Results of T-test analysis also revealed that there were significant mean differences in student's science achievement and their knowledge including physics, Chemistry, Biology and Earth science subjects and reasoning skills. A stepwise regression analysis significantly explained the variants of science achievement values knowledge and reasoning ability with large sciences.

CONCLUSION

The study of related literature has helped the investigator to have a clear perspective of the problem chosen for the present investigation. Keeping abreast of the work done in the field, the researcher has formulated the hypotheses for the present study. Designing the method of research, description of the variables, sample selection, selection of suitable tools, administration and scoring methods of responses have been undertaken based on the review which is discussed in the succeeding chapter. ❐

8

Desigh of the Study and the Method of Investigation

The chapter gives an overall picture of the design of the study, research tools used for the study, nature and selection of the sample and a brief description of the procedure adopted for collection of data in the light of other research studies.

STATEMENT OF THE PROBLEM

The present study is entitled as, *"A study on Cooperative learning and Achievement in Chemistry of higher secondary school students in Vellore district"*.

HYPOTHESES OF THE STUDY

1. The level of cooperative learning of higher secondary school students is moderate in nature.
2. The level of achievement in Chemistry of higher secondary school students is moderate in nature.
3. There is no significant difference in Cooperative learning of higher secondary school students based on gender.
4. There is no significant difference in achievement in Chemistry of higher secondary school students based on gender.

5. There is no significant difference in Cooperative learning of higher secondary school students based on types of management.
6. There is no significant difference in achievement in Chemistry of higher secondary school students based on types of management.
7. There is no significant difference in Cooperative learning of higher secondary school students based on types of family.
8. There is no significant difference in achievement in Chemistry of higher secondary school students based on types of family.
9. There is no significant difference in Cooperative learning of higher secondary school students based on medium of learning.
10. There is no significant difference in achievement in Chemistry of higher secondary school students based on medium of learning.
11. There is no significant difference in Cooperative learning of higher secondary school students based on father's educational qualification.
12. There is no significant difference in achievement in Chemistry of higher secondary school students based father's educational qualification.
13. There is no significant difference in Cooperative learning of higher secondary school students based on father's occupation.
14. There is no significant difference in achievement in Chemistry of higher secondary school students based on father's occupation.
15. There is no significant difference in Cooperative learning of higher secondary school students based on mother's educational qualification.
16. There is no significant difference in achievement in Chemistry of higher secondary school students based on mother's educational qualification.
17. There is no significant difference in Cooperative learning of higher secondary school students based on mother's occupation.
18. There is no significant difference in achievement in Chemistry of higher secondary school students based on mother's occupation.
19. There is no significant difference in Cooperative learning of higher secondary school students based on their fields of interest.
20. There is no significant difference in achievement in Chemistry of higher secondary school students based on their fields of interest.
21. There is no significant difference in Cooperative learning of higher secondary school students based on locality of house.
22. There is no significant difference in achievement in Chemistry of higher secondary school students based on locality of house.
23. There is no significant difference in Cooperative learning of higher secondary school students based on the mode of transport.
24. There is no significant difference in achievement in Chemistry of higher secondary school students based on the mode of transport.

25. There is no significant difference in Cooperative learning of higher secondary school students based on family monthly income.
26. There is no significant difference in achievement in Chemistry of higher secondary school students based on family monthly income.
27. There is no significant difference in Cooperative learning of higher secondary school students based on their wake up time during school days.
28. There is no significant difference in achievement in Chemistry of higher secondary school students based on their wake up time during school days.
29. There is no significant difference in Cooperative learning of higher secondary school students based on their usage of mobile phones.
30. There is no significant difference in achievement in Chemistry of higher secondary school students based on their usage of mobile phones.
31. There is no significant difference in Cooperative learning of higher secondary school students based on learning through tuition.
32. There is no significant difference in achievement in Chemistry of higher secondary school students based on learning through tuition.
33. There is no significant relationship between cooperative learning and achievement in Chemistry of higher secondary school students.

TOOLS AND TECHNIQUES USED

Researcher has used two important tools to identify the Cooperative learning and Achievement in Chemistry of higher secondary school students. They are

1. Cooperative learning assessment scale by the researcher, S. Kalpana and Mr. D. Arnold Robinson (2015)
2. Achievement in Chemistry assessment scale by the researcher, S. Kalpana and Mr. D. Arnold Robinson (2015)

COOPERATIVE LEARNING ASSESSMENT SCALE (CLAS)

Description of the Tool

Cooperative learning assessment scale was constructed and standardized by the researcher. This Cooperative learning assessment scale consists of 43 statements in which 25 of them are Positive and 18 of them are Negative statements. These statements were framed based on three dimensions namely interest of the students, influence of peer group and importance of teaching methodologies towards the process of cooperative learning. Each statement in this cooperative learning assessment scale has four alternatives responses viz. "Strongly Agree", "Agree", "Disagree", "Strongly Disagree". The maximum score for this scale is 129 and minimum is Zero. The average time for completing the scale is around 30 minutes.

TABL.8.1: Showing the Nature and List of Items of Cooperative learning Assessment Scale

POSITIVE (25)	1,2,3,7,8,9,10,13,14,15,16,18,19,20,21,22,25,29,30, 32,34,36,38,40,42
NEGATIVE (18)	4,5,6,11,12,17,23,24,26,27,28,31,33,35,37,39,41,43

ADMINISTRATION OF THE COOPERATIVE LEARNING ASSESSMENT SCALE

The Cooperative learning assessment scale was administrated to the respondents in groups in the regular classroom situation. The instruction provided on the first page of the scale booklet is by self-explanatory. Reading of the instructions by the examiner to the group however ensures better conditions for responding to the items of the scale. The answers were recorded by the respondent on the questionnaire protocol.

The time required for completing the scale items are between 20 minutes and 30 minutes classification sought by the higher secondary Chemistry students regarding any item was handled by the examiner through encouraging the respondents. In this way the administration procedure was carried out.

SCORING PROCEDURE

The final form of the questionnaire consists of 43 items. This assessment scale calls for a graded response to each statement on a four point scale. The points are usually denoted by "Strongly Agree", "Agree", "Disagree", "Strongly Disagree". The different points on the scale are assigned arbitrary weights for example 3,2,1 and 0 in the order of "Strongly Agree" response to "Strongly Disagree" response for all the statements. The total scores for an individual can be obtained by adding his/her scores for all the individual items (summated ratings). In this way all the items in the questionnaire should be scored. The maximum score for this questionnaire is 129 and the minimum score is 0.

TABLE. 8.2: Showing the Scoring Procedure Based on Response Given by the Students

Response	Positive	Negative
Strongly Agree	3	0
Agree	2	1
Disagree	1	2
Strongly Disagree	0	3

ACHIEVEMENT IN CHEMISTRY ASSESSMENT SCALE

Description of the Tool

Achievement in Chemistry assessment scale was constructed and standardized by the researcher. This Achievement in Chemistry assessment scale consists of 25 questions which are framed from 11th standard 2nd Mid-term Chemistry syllabus.

Each question in this achievement in Chemistry assessment scale have objective responses. The maximum score for this scale is 25 and minimum is Zero. The average time for completing the scale is around 10 minutes.

ADMINISTRATION OF THE ACHIEVEMENT IN CHEMISTRY ASSESSMENT SCALE

The Achievement in Chemistry assessment scale was administrated to the respondents in groups in the regular classroom situation. The instruction provided on the first page of the scale booklet is by self-explanatory. Reading of the instructions by the examiner to the group however ensures better conditions for responding to the items of the scale. The answers were recorded by the respondent on the questionnaire protocol.

The time required for completing the scale items are between 5 minutes and 10 minutes classification sought by the higher secondary Chemistry students regarding any item was handled by the examiner through encouraging the respondents. In this way the administration procedure was carried out.

TABLE. 8.3: Scoring Procedure of Achievement in Chemistry Assessment Scale

Response	Scores
Correct Answer	1
Wrong Answer	0

PILOT STUDY

A pilot study was conducted in the month of November on a small group of 50 higher secondary Chemistry students representing the whole population. This was done to check the reliability and validity of the tools used in the present study.

RELIABILITY AND VALIDITY OF TOOL

Reliability of Cooperative Learning Assessment Scale

Reliability refers to the consistency with which a test measures, whatever it measures. The concept of reliability suggests both stability and consistency of measurement. The investigator calculated the reliability by using split half method and was found to be 0.758.

Validity of Cooperative Learning Assessment Scale

The Cooperative learning assessment scale has content validity. The Cooperative learning assessment scale was given to the experts in order to find out its content validity. The experts agreed that the items in this assessment scale provided adequate coverage about the concept-Cooperative learning. The intrinsic validity of the tools was established by taking the square root of relation and was to found to 0.870.

Reliability of Achievement in Chemistry Assessment Scale

Reliability refers to the consistency with which a test measures, whatever it measures. The concept of reliability suggests both stability and consistency of measurement. The investigator calculated the reliability by using split half method and was found to be 0.88.

Validity of Achievement in Chemistry Assessment Scale

The achievement in Chemistry assessment scale has content validity. The achievement in Chemistry assessment scale was given to the experts in order to find out its content validity. The experts agreed that the items in this assessment scale provided adequate coverage about the concept-achievement in Chemistry. The intrinsic validity of the tools was established by taking the square root of relation and was to found to 0.95.

Selection of the Sample

Random sampling technique was used for selection of sample. The XI standard students from different status namely Government, Government-Aided and Private higher secondary school of Vellore city were selected as sample. Total numbers of students selected for this research are given in the following table.

TABLE. 8.4: Distribution of the Sample Based on Type of Management and Gender

Types of School	Gender		Total
	Male	Female	
Government	40	70	110
Government Aided	54	53	107
Private	57	46	103
Total	**151**	**169**	**320**

MAIN STUDY

The validated tools were used for the main study to collect the necessary data through survey method. The study was carried out among higher secondary Chemistry students in Vellore district, Tamil Nadu. In this investigation, the main purpose is to study cooperative learning and achievement in Chemistry among higher secondary students.

STATISTICAL TECHNIQUES USED IN THIS STUDY

Suitable descriptive, differential and correlation statistical techniques were used in the interpretation of the data to draw out a more meaningful picture of results from the collected data. In the present study the following statistical measures were used:

- Mean
- Standard Deviation
- Critical Ratio
- ANOVA
- Correlation

CONCLUSION

Adopting the methods and procedures discussed earlier in this chapter, tests were administered and scored. The various statistical techniques were implemented to analyze and systematize the data that were obtained through the tests in finding out the Cooperative learning, and Achievement among higher secondary Chemistry students. Further the results are discussed in the light of hypotheses formulated and present interpretations of the data collected in the next chapter.

❐

9

Analysis and Interpretation of the Data

Data analysis is a practice in which raw data is ordered and organized so that useful information can be extracted from it. The process of organizing and thinking about data is key to understanding what the data does and does not contain. There are a variety of ways in which people can approach data analysis, and it is notoriously easy to manipulate data during the analysis phase to push certain conclusions of agenda.

According to Gay (1976), "Analysis of the data is important as any other component of the research process". This chapter describes analysis of the data and testing of the hypotheses that have been framed on the basis of the objectives, using appropriate statistical techniques.

The following areas have been analyzed by the researcher.

1. Descriptive Analysis

Descriptive statistics enables us to present the data in a more meaningful way, which allows simpler interpretation of the data. A set of brief descriptive coefficients that summarizes a given data set, which can either be a representation of the entire population or a sample.

2. Differential Analysis

Differential analysis is a method of comparing two or more business alternatives to each other in an attempt to decide which the right choice is.

3. Correlation Analysis

Correlation is a statistical measure that indicates the extent to which two or more variables fluctuate together. A positive correlation indicates the extent to which those variables increase or decrease in parallel; a negative correlation indicates the extent to which one variable increases as the other decreases. When the fluctuation of one variable reliably predicts a similar fluctuation in another variable.

DESCRIPTIVE ANALYSIS

COOPERATIVE LEARNING OF HIGHER SECONDARY SCHOOL STUDENTS

Hypothesis-1

The level of cooperative learning of higher secondary school students is moderate in nature.

TABLE. 9.1: Showing the Levels of Cooperative Learning among Higher Secondary School Students

Variable	Range	Level	Frequency	Percentage
Cooperative learning	Below 81	Low	82	25.6
	82-97	Moderate	151	47.2
	Above 98	High	87	27.2

INFERENCE

From the above table, it is clear that the level of cooperative learning of higher secondary school students is moderate (47.2) in nature.

Hence, the hypothesis - 1 is accepted.

ACHIEVEMENT IN CHEMISTRY OF HIGHER SECONDARY SCHOOL STUDENTS

Hypothesis-2

The level of achievement in Chemistry of higher secondary school students is moderate in nature.

TABLE .9.2: Showing the Levels of Achievement in Chemistry among Higher Secondary School Students

Variable	Range	Level	Frequency	Percentage
Achievement in Chemistry	Below 11	Low	96	30.0
	12-17	Moderate	135	42.2
	Above 18	High	89	27.8

INFERENCE

From the table, it is clear that the level of achievement in Chemistry of higher secondary school students is moderate (42.2) in nature.

Hence, the hypothesis - 2 is accepted.

INFLUENCE OF GENDER ON COOPERATIVE LEARNING

Hypothesis-3

There is no significant difference in cooperative learning of higher secondary school students based on gender.

TABLE.9.3: Showing the Significant Difference between the mean Scores of Cooperative learning of Higher Secondary School Students with Regard to Gender

Variable	Gender	N	Mean	SD	't' Value	L.S
Cooperative learning	Male	151	83.85	11.972	8.155	0.01
	Female	169	93.70	9.606		

INFERENCE

The calculated 't' Value (8.155) is greater than the table 't' Value (2.58) at 0.01 level of significance, showing that there is significant difference between the mean scores of cooperative learning of higher secondary school students with respect to gender.

Hence, the hypothesis - 3 is rejected.

Moreover, female students have significantly higher cooperative learning than male students.

INFLUENCE OF GENDER ON ACHIEVEMENT IN CHEMISTRY

Hypothesis-4

There is no significant difference in achievement in Chemistry of higher secondary school students based on gender.

TABLE.9.4: Showing the Significant Difference between the mean Scores of Achievement in Chemistry of Higher Secondary School Students with Regard to Gender

Variable	Gender	N	Mean	SD	't' Value	L.S
Achievement in Chemistry	Male	151	12.72	3.721	7.704	0.01
	Female	169	16.27	4.439		

INFERENCE

The calculated 't' Value (7.704) is greater than the table 't' Value (2.58) at 0.01 level of significance, showing that there is significant difference between the mean scores of achievement in Chemistry with respect to gender.

Hence, the hypothesis - 4 is rejected.

Moreover, female students have significantly higher achievement in Chemistry than male students.

INFLUENCE OF TYPE OF MANAGEMENT ON COOPERATIVE LEARNING

Hypothesis-5

There is no significant difference in cooperative learning of higher secondary school students based on type of management.

TABLE.9.5: ANOVA Showing the Significance of the Difference between the mean Scores of Cooperative Learning of the Students Studying at the Higher Secondary School with Respect to Type of Management

Variable		Sum of Squares	DF	Mean Squares	F Value	L.S
Cooperative learning	Between Groups	2866.457	2	1433.228	10.850	0.01
	Within groups	41874.743	317	132.097		
	Total	**44741.200**	**319**			

INFERENCE

The calculated 'F' Value (10.850) is greater than the table Value (3.02) at 0.01 level of significance, showing that there is significant difference between the mean scores of cooperative learning of higher secondary students with respect to type of management.

Further calculations have been made to check the difference between types of management.

TABLE.9.5 (A) Showing the Significant Difference between the mean Scores of Cooperative Learning of Higher Secondary School Students with Regard to Type of Management

Variable	Type of Management	N	Mean	SD	't' Value	L.S
Cooperative learning	Government Vs Government-Aided	108	93.06	11.510	3.041	0.01
		107	88.06	12.617		
	Government Vs Private	108	93.06	11.510	4.780	0.01
		105	85.93	10.202		
	Government-Aided Vs Private	107	88.06	12.617	1.346	NS
		105	85.93	10.202		

INFERENCE

From the above table the following inferences have been made.

In the first case, the calculated 't' value (3.041) is greater than the table 't' value (2.58) at 0.01 level of significance showing that there is significant difference between students studying in Government and Government-Aided higher secondary school with regard to their Cooperative learning.

In the second case, the calculated 't' value (4.780) is greater than the table 't' value (2.58) at 0.01 level of significance showing that there is significant difference between students studying in Government and Private higher secondary school with regard to their Cooperative learning.

In the third case, the calculated 't' value (1.346) is lesser than the table 't' value (1.96) at 0.05 level of significance showing that there is no significant difference between students studying in Government-Aided and Private higher secondary school with regard to their cooperative learning.

Hence, the hypothesis – 5 is partially verified.

From this verification student's studying in government higher secondary school exhibits higher cooperative learning.

INFLUENCE OF TYPE OF MANAGEMENT ON ACHIEVEMENT IN CHEMISTRY

Hypothesis-6

There is no significant difference in achievement in Chemistry of higher secondary school students based on type of management.

TABLE.9.6: ANOVA Showing the Significance of the Difference between the mean Scores of Achievement in Chemistry of the Students Studying at the Higher Secondary School with Respect to Type of Management

Variable		Sum of Squares	DF	Mean Squares	F Value	L.S
Achievement in Chemistry	Between Groups	1175.542	2	587.771	35.709	0.01
	Within groups	5217.830	317	16.460		
	Total	**6393.372**	**319**			

INFERENCE

The calculated 'F' Value (35.709) is greater than the table Value (3.02) at 0.01 level of significance showing that there is significant difference between the mean scores of achievement in Chemistry of higher secondary school students with respect to type of management.

Further calculations have been made to check the difference among students studying in various type of management.

TABLE.9.6 (A) Showing the Significant Difference between the mean Score of Achievement in Chemistry of Higher Secondary School Students with Regards to Type of Management

Variable	Type of Management	N	Mean	SD	't' Value	L.S
Achievement in Chemistry	Government Vs Government-Aided	108	17.23	4.374	7.374	0.01
		107	12.82	4.393		
	Government Vs Private	108	17.23	4.374	6.690	0.01
		105	13.68	3.289		
	Government-Aided Vs Private	107	12.82	4.393	1.600	NS
		105	13.68	3.289		

NFERENCE

From the above table the following inferences have been made.

In the first case, the calculated 't' value (7.374) is greater than the table 't' value (2.58) at 0.01 level of significance showing that there is significant difference between students studying in Government and Government-Aided higher secondary school with regard to their achievement in Chemistry.

In the second case, the calculated 't' value (6.690) is greater than the table 't' value (2.58) at 0.01 level of significance showing that there is significant difference between students studying in Government and Private higher secondary school with regard to their achievement in Chemistry.

In the third case, the calculated 't' value (1.600) is lesser than the table 't' value (1.96) at 0.05 level of significance showing that there is no significant difference between students studying in Government-Aided and Private higher secondary school with regard to their achievement in Chemistry.

Hence, the hypothesis – 6 is partially verified.

From this verification, student's studying in Government higher secondary school excel in achievement in Chemistry than that of other schools.

INFLUENCE OF TYPE OF FAMILY ON COOPERATIVE LEARNING

Hypothesis-7

There is no significant difference in cooperative learning of higher secondary school students based on type of family.

TABLE.9.7: Showing the Significant Difference between the mean Scores of Cooperative Learning of Higher Secondary School Students with Regard to Type of Family

Variable	Type of family	N	Mean	SD	't' value	L.S
Cooperative learning	Nuclear	273	89.75	11.473	2.588	0.01
	Joint	47	84.96	13.201		

INFERENCE

The calculated 't' Value (2.588) is greater than the table 't' Value (2.58) at 0.01 level of significance, showing that there is significant difference between the mean scores of cooperative learning of higher secondary school students with respect to type of family.

Hence, the hypothesis - 7 is rejected.

Moreover, students from nuclear family have significantly higher cooperative learning than joint family students.

INFLUENCE OF TYPE OF FAMILY ON ACHIEVEMENT IN CHEMISTRY

Hypothesis-8

There is no significant difference in achievement in Chemistry of higher secondary school students based on type of family.

TABLE.9.8: Showing the Significant Difference between the mean Score of Achievement in Chemistry of Higher Secondary School Students with Regard to Type of Family

Variable	Type of family	N	Mean	SD	't' value	L.S
Achievement in Chemistry	Nuclear	273	14.79	4.522	1.976	0.05
	Joint	47	13.40	4.047		

INFERENCE

The calculated 't' Value (1.976) is greater than the table 't' Value (1.96) at 0.05 level of significance showing that there is significant difference between the mean scores of achievement in Chemistry of higher secondary school students with respect to type of family.

Hence, the hypothesis - 8 is rejected.

Moreover, students from nuclear family have significantly higher achievement in Chemistry than joint family students.

INFLUENCE OF MEDIUM OF LEARNING ON COOPERATIVE LEARNING

Hypothesis-9

There is no significant difference in cooperative learning of higher secondary school students based on medium of learning.

TABLE.9.9: Showing the Significant Difference between the mean Scores of Cooperative Learning of Higher Secondary School Students with Regard to Medium of Learning

Variable	Medium of learning	N	Mean	SD	't' value	L.S
Cooperative learning	Tamil	107	91.98	12.611	3.183	0.01
	English	213	87.58	11.181		

INFERENCE

The calculated 't' Value (3.183) is greater than the table 't' Value (2.58) at 0.01 level of significance, showing that there is significant difference between the mean scores of cooperative learning of higher secondary school students with respect to medium of learning.

Hence, the hypothesis - 9 is rejected.

Moreover, Tamil medium students have significantly higher cooperative learning than English medium students.

INFLUENCE OF MEDIUM OF LEARNING ON ACHIEVEMENT IN CHEMISTRY

Hypothesis-10

There is no significant difference in achievement in Chemistry of higher secondary school students based on medium of learning.

TABLE.9.10: Showing the Significant Difference between the mean Scores of Achievement in Chemistry of Higher Secondary School Students with regard to Medium of Learning

Variable	Medium of learning	N	Mean	SD	't' value	L.S
Achievement in Chemistry	Tamil	107	16.15	5.354	4.871	0.01
	English	213	13.76	3.706		

INFERENCE

The calculated 't' Value (4.871) is greater than the table 't' Value (2.58) at 0.01 level of significance, showing that there is significant difference between the mean scores of achievement in Chemistry of higher secondary school students with respect to medium of learning.

Hence, the hypothesis - 10 is rejected.

Moreover, Tamil medium students have significantly higher achievement in Chemistry than English medium students.

INFLUENCE OF EDUCATIONAL QUALIFICATION OF FATHER ON COOPERATIVE LEARNING

Hypothesis-11

There is no significant difference in cooperative learning of higher secondary school students based on father's educational qualification.

TABLE.9.11: ANOVA Showing the Significance of the Difference between the mean Scores of Cooperative Learning of the Students Studying at the Higher Secondary School with Respect to educational Qualification of Father

Variable		Sum of Squares	DF	Mean Squares	F Value	L.S
Cooperative learning	Between groups	82.619	2	41.309	0.293	NS
	Within groups	44658.581	317	140.879		
	Total	**44741.200**	**319**			

INFERENCE

The calculated 'F' Value (0.293) is lesser than the table Value (3.02) at 0.05 level of significance, showing that there is no significant difference between the mean scores of cooperative learning of higher secondary school students with respect to father's educational qualification.

Hence, the hypothesis - 11 is accepted.

INFLUENCE OF EDUCATIONAL QUALIFICATION OF FATHER ON ACHIEVEMENT IN CHEMISTRY

Hypothesis-12

There is no significant difference in achievement in Chemistry of higher secondary school students based on father's educational qualification.

TABLE.9.12: ANOVA Showing the Significance of the Difference between the mean Scores of Achievement in Chemistry of the Students Studying at the Higher Secondary School with Respect to Educational Qualification of Father

Variable		Sum of Squares	DF	Mean Squares	F Value	L.S
Achievement in Chemistry	Between groups	56.861	2	28.431	1.422	NS
	Within groups	6336.511	317	19.989		
	Total	**6393.372**	**319**			

INFERENCE

The calculated 'F' Value (1.422) is lesser than the table Value (3.02) at 0.05 level of significance, showing that there is no significant difference between the mean scores of achievement in Chemistry of higher secondary school students with respect to father's educational qualification.

Hence, the hypothesis - 12 is accepted.

INFLUENCE OF OCCUPATION OF FATHER ON COOPERATIVE LEARNING

Hypothesis-13

There is no significant difference in cooperative learning of higher secondary school students based on father's occupation.

TABLE.9.13: ANOVA Showing the Significance of the Difference between the mean Scores of Cooperative Learning of the Students Studying at the Higher Secondary School with Respect to Occupation of Father

Variable	Father's Occupation	N	Mean	SD	't' Value	L.S
Cooperative learning	Private	255	89.40	12.256	1.047	NS
	Government	65	87.68	10.027		

INFERENCE

The calculated 't' Value (1.047) is lesser than the table 't' Value (1.96) at 0.05 level of significance, showing that there is no significant difference between the mean scores of cooperative learning of higher secondary school students with respect to father's occupation.

Hence, the hypothesis - 13 is accepted.

INFLUENCE OF OCCUPATION OF FATHER ON ACHIEVEMENT IN CHEMISTRY

Hypothesis-14

There is no significant difference in achievement in Chemistry of higher secondary school students based on father's occupation.

TABLE.9.14: ANOVA Showing the Significance of the Difference between the mean Scores of Achievement in Chemistry of the Students Studying at the Higher Secondary School with Respect to Occupation of Father

Variable	Father's Occupation	N	Mean	SD	't' Value	L.S
Achievement in Chemistry	Private	255	14.47	4.589	0.981	NS
	Government	65	15.08	4.001		

INFERENCE

The calculated 't' Value (0.981) is less than the table 't' Value (1.96) at 0.05 level of significance, showing that there is no significant difference between the mean scores of achievement in Chemistry of higher secondary school students with respect to father's occupation.

Hence, the hypothesis - 14 is accepted.

INFLUENCE OF EDUCATIONAL QUALIFICATION OF MOTHER ON COOPERATIVE LEARNING

Hypothesis-15

There is no significant difference in cooperative learning of higher secondary school students based on mother's educational qualification.

TABLE.9.15: ANOVA Showing the Significance of the Difference between the mean Scores of Cooperative Learning of the Students Studying at the Higher Secondary School with Respect to educational Qualification of Mother

Variable		Sum of Squares	DF	Mean Squares	F Value	L.S
Cooperative learning	Between groups	177.485	2	88.743	0.631	NS
	Within groups	44563.715	317	140.580		
	Total	**44741.200**	**319**			

INFERENCE

The calculated 'F' Value (0.631) is lesser than the table Value (3.02) at 0.05 level of significance, showing that there is no significant difference between the mean scores of cooperative learning of higher secondary school students with respect to mother's educational qualification.

Hence, the hypothesis - 15 is accepted.

INFLUENCE OF EDUCATIONAL QUALIFICATION OF MOTHER ON ACHIEVEMENT IN CHEMISTRY

Hypothesis-16

There is no significant difference in achievement in Chemistry of higher secondary school students based on mother's educational qualification.

TABLE.9.16: ANOVA Showing the Significance of the Difference between the mean Scores of Achievement in Chemistry of the Students Studying at the Higher Secondary School with respect to Educational Qualification of Mother

Variable		Sum of Squares	DF	Mean Squares	F Value	L.S
Achievement in Chemistry	Between groups	74.542	2	37.271	1.870	NS
	Within groups	6318.830	317	19.933		
	Total	**6393.372**	**319**			

INFERENCE

The calculated 'F' Value (1.870) is lesser than the table Value (3.02) at 0.05 level of significance, showing that there is no significant difference between the mean scores of achievement in Chemistry of higher secondary school students with respect to mother's educational qualification.

Hence, the hypothesis - 16 is accepted.

INFLUENCE OF OCCUPATION OF MOTHER ON COOPERATIVE LEARNING

Hypothesis-17

There is no significant difference in cooperative learning of higher secondary school students based on mother's occupation.

TABLE.9.17: ANOVA Showing the Significance of the Difference between the mean Scores of Cooperative Learning of the Students Studying at the Higher Secondary School with Respect to Occupation of Mother

Variable		Sum of Squares	DF	Mean Squares	F Value	L.S
Cooperative learning	Between groups	108.745	2	54.372	0.386	NS
	Within groups	44632.455	317	140.796		
	Total	**44741.200**	**319**			

INFERENCE

The calculated 'F' Value (0.386) is lesser than the table Value (3.02) at 0.05 level of significance, showing that there is no significant difference between the mean scores of cooperative learning of higher secondary school students with respect to mother's occupation.

Hence, the hypothesis - 17 is accepted.

INFLUENCE OF OCCUPATION OF MOTHER ON ACHIEVEMENT IN CHEMISTRY

Hypothesis-18

There is no significant difference in achievement in Chemistry of higher secondary school students based on mother's occupation.

TABLE.9.18: ANOVA Showing the Significance of the Difference between the mean Scores of Achievement in Chemistry of the Students Studying at the Higher Secondary School with Respect to Occupation of Mother

Variable		Sum of Squares	DF	Mean Squares	F Value	L.S
Achievement in Chemistry	Between groups	73.290	2	36.645	1.838	NS
	Within groups	6320.082	317	19.937		
	Total	**6393.372**	**319**			

INFERENCE

The calculated 'F' Value (1.838) is lesser than the table Value (3.02) at 0.05 level of significance, showing that there is no significant difference between the mean scores of achievement in Chemistry of higher secondary school students with respect to mother's occupation.

Hence, the hypothesis - 18 is accepted.

INFLUENCE OF FIELD OF INTEREST ON COOPERATIVE LEARNING

Hypothesis-19

There is no significant difference in cooperative learning of higher secondary school students based on their field of interest.

TABLE.9.19: ANOVA Showing the Significance of the Difference between the mean Scores of Cooperative Learning of the Students Studying at the Higher Secondary School with Respect to Field of Interest

Variable		Sum of Squares	DF	Mean Squares	F Value	L.S
Cooperative learning	Between Groups	955.244	2	477.622	3.458	0.05
	Within groups	43785.956	317	138.126		
	Total	**44741.200**	**319**			

INFERENCE

From the above table, it is clear that calculated F-value (3.458) is greater than the table value (3.02) at 0.05 level of significance, showing that there is significant difference in cooperative learning of higher secondary school students based on their field of interest.

Further calculations have been made to find the difference.

TABLE.9.19 (A) Showing the Significant Difference between the mean Scores of Cooperative Learning of Higher Secondary School Students with Related to field of Interest

Variable	Interest	N	Mean	SD	't' Value	L.S
Cooperative learning	Music vs Sports	132	90.09	10.741	2.311	0.05
		107	86.63	12.428		
	Music vs Reading Books	132	90.09	10.741	0.289	NS
		81	90.56	12.401		
	Sports vs Reading Books	107	86.63	12.428	2.149	0.05
		81	90.56	12.401		

INFERENCE

From the above table the following inferences have been made.

In the first case, the calculated 't' value (2.311) is greater than the table 't' value (1.96) at 0.05 level of significance, showing that there is significant difference between higher secondary school student's interest in Music and Sports with regard to their cooperative learning.

In the second case, the calculated 't' value (0.289) is lesser than the table 't' value (1.96) at 0.05 level of significance, showing that there is no significant difference between higher secondary school student's interest in Music and Reading books with regard to their cooperative learning.

In the third case, the calculated 't' value (2.149) is greater than the table 't' value (1.96) at 0.05 level of significance, showing that there is significant difference between higher secondary school student's interest in Sports and Reading books with regard to their cooperative learning.

Hence, the hypothesis – 19 is partially verified.

INFLUENCE OF FIELD OF INTEREST ON ACHIEVEMENT IN CHEMISTRY

Hypothesis-20

There is no significant difference in achievement in Chemistry of higher secondary school students based on their field of interest.

TABLE.9.20: ANOVA Showing the Significance of the Difference between the mean Scores of Achievement in Chemistry of the Students Studying at the Higher Secondary School with Respect to Field of Interest

Variable		Sum of Squares	DF	Mean Squares	F Value	L.S
Achievement in Chemistry	Between Groups	296.006	2	148.003	7.695	0.01
	Within groups	6097.365	317	19.235		
	Total	**6393.372**	**319**			

INFERENCE

From the above table, it is clear that calculated F-value (7.695) is greater than that table value (3.02) at 0.01 level of significance, showing that there is significant difference in achievement in Chemistry among higher secondary school students based on their field of interest.

Further calculations have been made to find the difference among the field of interest.

TABLE.9.20 (A) Showing the Significant Difference between the mean Scores of Achievement in Chemistry of Higher Secondary School Students with Related to field of Interest

Variable	Interest	N	Mean	SD	't' Value	L.S
Achievement in Chemistry	Music Vs Sports	132	15.27	4.520	3.638	0.01
		107	13.23	4.032		
	Music Vs Reading Books	132	15.27	4.520	0.002	NS
		81	15.27	4.607		
	Sports Vs Reading Books	107	13.23	4.032	3.226	0.01
		81	15.27	4.607		

INFERENCE

From the above table the following inferences have been made.

In the first case, the calculated 't' value (3.638) is greater than the table 't' value (2.58) at 0.01 level of significance, showing that there is significant difference between higher secondary school student's interest in Music and Sports with regard to their achievement in Chemistry.

In the second case, the calculated 't' value (0.002) is lesser than the table 't' value (1.96) at 0.05 level of significance, showing that there is no significant difference between higher secondary school student's interest in Music and Reading books with regard to their achievement in Chemistry.

In the third case, the calculated 't' value (3.226) is greater than the table 't' value (2.58) at 0.01 level of significance, showing that there is significant difference between higher secondary school student's interest in Sports and Reading books with regard to their achievement in Chemistry.

Hence, the hypothesis – 20 is partially verified.

INFLUENCE OF LOCALITY OF HOUSE ON COOPERATIVE LEARNING

Hypothesis-21

There is no significant difference in cooperative learning of higher secondary school students based on locality of house.

TABLE.9.21: Showing the Significant Difference between the mean Scores of Cooperative Learning of Higher Secondary School Students with regard to Locality of House

Variable	Locality of House	N	Mean	SD	't' Value	L.S
Cooperative learning	Rural	89	86.99	11.681	1.941	NS
	Urban	231	89.84	11.834		

INFERENCE

The calculated 't' Value (1.941) is lesser than the table 't' Value (1.96) at 0.05 level of significance, showing that there is no significant difference between the mean scores of cooperative learning of higher secondary school students with respect to locality of house.

Hence, the hypothesis - 21 is accepted.

INFLUENCE OF LOCALITY OF HOUSE ON ACHIEVEMENT IN CHEMISTRY

Hypothesis-22

There is no significant difference in achievement in Chemistry of higher secondary school students based on locality of house.

TABLE. 9.22: Showing the Significant Difference between the mean Scores of Achievement in Chemistry of Higher Secondary School Students with Regard to Locality of House

Variable	Locality of House	N	Mean	SD	't' Value	L.S
Achievement in Chemistry	Rural	89	14.22	4.322	0.907	NS
	Urban	231	14.73	4.536		

INFERENCE

The calculated 't' Value (0.907) is lesser than the table 't' Value (1.96) at 0.05 level of significance, showing that there is no significant difference between the mean scores of achievement in Chemistry of higher secondary school students with respect to locality of house.

Hence, the hypothesis - 22 is accepted.

INFLUENCE OF MODE OF TRANSPORT ON COOPERATIVE LEARNING

Hypothesis-23

There is no significant difference in cooperative learning of higher secondary school students based on the mode of transport.

TABLE.9.23: ANOVA Showing the Significance of the Difference between the mean Scores of Cooperative Learning of the Students Studying at the Higher Secondary School with Respect to mode of Transport

Variable		Sum of Squares	DF	Mean Squares	F Value	L.S
Cooperative learning	Between Groups	251.673	2	125.836	0.897	NS
	Within groups	44489.527	317	140.346		
	Total	**44741.200**	**319**			

INFERENCE

The calculated 'F' Value (0.897) is lesser than the table Value (3.02) at 0.05 level of significance, showing that there is no significant difference between the mean scores of cooperative learning of higher secondary school students with respect to mode of transport.

Hence, the hypothesis - 23 is accepted.

INFLUENCE OF MODE OF TRANSPORT ON ACHIEVEMENT IN CHEMISTRY

Hypothesis-24

There is no significant difference in achievement in Chemistry of higher secondary school students based on the mode of transport.

TABLE.9.24: ANOVA Showing the Significance of the Difference between the mean Scores of Achievement in Chemistry of the Students Studying at the Higher Secondary School with Respect to mode of Transport

Variable		Sum of Squares	DF	Mean Squares	F Value	L.S
Achievement in Chemistry	Between Groups	9.831	2	4.916	0.244	NS
	Within groups	6383.541	317	20.137		
	Total	**6393.372**	**319**			

INFERENCE

The calculated 'F' Value (0.244) is lesser than the table Value (3.02) at 0.05 level of significance, showing that there is no significant difference between the mean scores of achievement in Chemistry of higher secondary school students with respect to mode of transport.

Hence, the hypothesis - 24 is accepted.

INFLUENCE OF FAMILY MONTHLY INCOME ON COOPERATIVE LEARNING

Hypothesis-25

There is no significant difference in cooperative learning of higher secondary school students based on family monthly income.

TABLE.9.25: ANOVA Showing the Significance of the Difference between the mean Scores of Cooperative Learning of the Students Studying at the Higher Secondary School with Respect to Family Monthly Income

Variable		Sum of Squares	DF	Mean Squares	F Value	L.S
Cooperative learning	Between Groups	378.857	2	189.429	1.354	NS
	Within groups	44362.343	317	139.944		
	Total	44741.200	319			

INFERENCE

The calculated 'F' Value (1.354) is lesser than the table Value (3.02) at 0.05 level of significance, showing that there is no significant difference between the mean scores of achievement in Chemistry of higher secondary school students with respect to family monthly income.

Hence, the hypothesis - 25 is accepted.

INFLUENCE OF FAMILY MONTHLY INCOME ON ACHIEVEMENT IN CHEMISTRY

Hypothesis-26

There is no significant difference in achievement in Chemistry of higher secondary school students based on family monthly income.

TABLE.9.26: ANOVA Showing the Significance of the Difference between the mean Scores of Achievement in Chemistry of the Students Studying at the Higher Secondary School with Respect to Family Monthly Income

Variable		Sum of Squares	DF	Mean Squares	F Value	L.S
Achievement in Chemistry	Between Groups	18.781	2	9.390	0.467	NS
	Within groups	6374.591	317	20.109		
	Total	**6393.372**	**319**			

INFERENCE

The calculated 'F' Value (0.467) is lesser than the table Value (3.02) at 0.05 level of significance, showing that there is no significant difference between the mean scores of achievement in Chemistry of higher secondary school students with respect to family monthly income.

Hence, the hypothesis - 26 is accepted.

INFLUENCE OF WAKE UP TIME ON COOPERATIVE LEARNING

Hypothesis-27

There is no significant difference in cooperative learning of higher secondary school students based on their wake up time during school days.

TABLE.9.27: Showing the Significant Difference between the mean Scores of Cooperative Learning of Higher Secondary School Students with Regard to wake up time During School days

Variable	Wake up Time	N	Mean	SD	't' Value	L.S
Cooperative learning	Before 6.00 Am	226	89.32	11.455	0.639	NS
	After 6.00 Am	94	88.39	12.769		

INFERENCE

The calculated 't' Value (0.639) is lesser than the table 't' Value (1.96) at 0.05 level of significance, showing that there is no significant difference between the mean scores of cooperative learning of higher secondary school students with respect to wake up time during school days.

Hence, the hypothesis - 27 is accepted.

INFLUENCE OF WAKE UP TIME ON ACHIEVEMENT IN CHEMISTRY

Hypothesis-28

There is no significant difference in achievement in Chemistry of higher secondary school students based on their wake up time during school days.

TABLE.9.28: Showing the Significant Difference between the mean Scores of Achievement in Chemistry of Higher Secondary School Students with Regard to wake up time During School Days

Variable	Wake up Time	N	Mean	SD	't' Value	L.S
Achievement in Chemistry	Before 6.00 Am	226	14.42	4.532	1.028	NS
	After 6.00 Am	94	14.99	4.339		

INFERENCE

The calculated 't' Value (1.028) is lesser than the table 't' Value (1.96) at 0.05 level of significance, showing that there is no significant difference between the mean scores of achievement in Chemistry of higher secondary school students with respect to wake up time during school days.

Hence, the hypothesis - 28 is accepted.

INFLUENCE OF USAGE OF MOBILE PHONES ON COOPERATIVE LEARNING

Hypothesis-29

There is no significant difference in cooperative learning of higher secondary school students based on their usage of mobile phones.

TABLE.9.29: ANOVA Showing the Significance of the Difference between the mean Scores of Cooperative Learning of the Students Studying at the Higher Secondary School with Respect to usage of Mobile Phones

Variable		Sum of Squares	DF	Mean Squares	F Value	L.S
Cooperative learning	Between Groups	538.802	2	269.401	1.932	NS
	Within groups	44202.398	317	139.440		
	Total	**44741.200**	**319**			

INFERENCE

The calculated 'F' Value (1.932) is lesser than the table Value (3.02) at 0.05 level of significance, showing that there is no significant difference between the mean scores of cooperative learning of higher secondary school students with respect to usage of mobile phones.

Hence, the hypothesis - 29 is accepted.

INFLUENCE OF USAGE OF MOBILE PHONES ON ACHIEVEMENT IN CHEMISTRY

Hypothesis-30

There is no significant difference in achievement in Chemistry of higher secondary school students based on their usage of mobile phones.

TABLE.9.30: ANOVA Showing the Significance of the Difference between the mean Scores of Achievement in Chemistry of the Students Studying at the Higher Secondary School with Respect to Usage of Mobile Phones

Variable		Sum of Squares	DF	Mean Squares	F Value	L.S
Achievement in Chemistry	Between Groups	109.669	2	54.835	2.766	NS
	Within groups	6283.703	317	19.822		
	Total	6393.372	319			

INFERENCE

The calculated 'F' Value (2.766) is lesser than the table Value (3.02) at 0.05 level of significance, showing that there is no significant difference between the mean scores of achievement in Chemistry of higher secondary school students with respect to usage of mobile phones.

Hence, the hypothesis - 30 is accepted.

INFLUENCE OF LEARNING THROUGH TUTION ON COOPERATIVE LEARNING

Hypothesis-31

There is no significant difference in cooperative learning of higher secondary school students based on learning through tuition.

TABLE.9.31: Showing the Significant Difference between the mean Scores of Cooperative Learning of Higher Secondary School Students with Regard to Learning through Tuition

Variable	Learning through Tuition	N	Mean	SD	't' Value	L.S
Cooperative learning	Yes	109	85.75	12.474	3.649	0.01
	No	211	90.75	11.157		

INFERENCE

The calculated 't' Value (3.649) is greater than the table 't' Value (2.58) at 0.01 level of significance, showing that there is significant difference between the mean scores of cooperative learning of higher secondary school students with respect to learning through tuition.

Hence, the hypothesis - 31 is rejected.

Moreover, students who do not attend tuitions have significantly higher cooperative learning than those who attend tuitions.

INFLUENCE OF LEARNING THROUGH TUTION ON ACHIEVEMENT IN CHEMISTRY

Hypothesis-32

There is no significant difference in achievement in Chemistry of higher secondary school students based on learning through tuition.

TABLE.9.32: Showing the Significant Difference between the mean Scores of Achievement in Chemistry of Higher Secondary School Students with Regard to Learning through Tuition

Variable	Learning through Tuition	N	Mean	SD	't' Value	L.S
Achievement in Chemistry	Yes	109	13.78	4.326	2.345	0.05
	No	211	15.01	4.506		

INFERENCE

The calculated 't' Value (2.345) is greater than the table 't' Value (1.96) at 0.05 level of significance, showing that there is significant difference between the mean scores of achievement in Chemistry of higher secondary school students with respect to learning through tuition.

Hence, the hypothesis - 32 is rejected.

Moreover, students who do not attend tuitions have significantly higher achievement in Chemistry than those who attend tuitions.

CORRELATION ANALYSIS

Hypothesis-33

There is no significant relationship between cooperative learning and achievement in Chemistry of higher secondary school students.

TABLE.9.33: Showing the Correlation between Cooperative Learning and Achievement in Chemistry of Higher Secondary School Students

Variable	N	Correlation	Significance level
Cooperative learning vs Achievement in Chemistry	320	0.481	0.01

INFERENCE

From the above table, it is observed that the calculated value is (0.481) indicates Positive correlation. It is clear that there is significant and positive correlation on the cooperative learning and achievement in Chemistry among higher secondary school students.

Hence, the hypothesis – 33 is rejected.

CONCLUSION

This chapter explain the analysis of data, testing of hypotheses and interpretation of the data. A brief report of the research study together which the major findings, educational implications and the suggestions for further research has been discussed in succeeding chapter.

❐

10

Summary, Findings and Conclusion

In this chapter the statement of the problem, descriptions of the procedure used in the investigation, the findings and conclusions are presented. In the light of the finding of the present study a few suggestions have been given as further research in the field.

STATEMENT OF THE PROBLEM

The researcher has framed the following topic as statements of the problem. "A study on cooperative learning and achievement in Chemistry of higher secondary school students in Vellore district".

OBJECTIVES OF THE STUDY

The following are the objectives formulated for the present study.

1. To find out the level of cooperative learning of higher secondary school students.
2. To find out the level of achievement in Chemistry of higher secondary school students.
3. To find out the significant difference in cooperative learning of higher secondary school students based on gender.

4. To find out the significant difference in achievement in Chemistry of higher secondary school students based on gender.
5. To find out the significant difference in cooperative learning of higher secondary school students based on type of management.
6. To find out the significant difference in achievement in Chemistry of higher secondary school students based on type of management.
7. To find out the significant difference in cooperative learning of higher secondary school students based on type of family.
8. To find out the significant difference in achievement in Chemistry of higher secondary school students based on type of family.
9. To find out the significant difference in cooperative learning of higher secondary school students based on medium of learning.
10. To find out the significant difference in achievement in Chemistry of higher secondary school students based on medium of learning.
11. To find out the significant difference in cooperative learning of higher secondary school students based on father's educational qualification.
12. To find out the significant difference in achievement in Chemistry of higher secondary school students based on father's educational qualification.
13. To find out the significant difference in cooperative learning of higher secondary school students based on father's occupation.
14. To find out the significant difference in achievement in Chemistry of higher secondary school students based on father's occupation.
15. To find out the significant difference in cooperative learning of higher secondary school students based on mother's educational qualification.
16. To find out the significant difference in achievement in Chemistry of higher secondary school students based on mother's educational qualification.
17. To find out the significant difference in cooperative learning of higher secondary school students based on mother's occupation.
18. To find out the significant difference in achievement in Chemistry of higher secondary school students based on mother's occupation.
19. To find out the significant difference in cooperative learning of higher secondary school students based on their field of interest.
20. To find out the significant difference in achievement in Chemistry of higher secondary school students based on their field of interest.
21. To find out the significant difference in cooperative learning of higher secondary school students based on locality of house.
22. To find out the significant difference in achievement in Chemistry of higher secondary school students based on locality of house.

23. To find out the significant difference in cooperative learning of higher secondary school students based on the mode of transport.
24. To find out the significant difference in achievement in Chemistry of higher secondary school students based on the mode of transport.
25. To find out the significant difference in cooperative learning of higher secondary school students based on family monthly income.
26. To find out the significant difference in achievement in Chemistry of higher secondary school students based on family monthly income.
27. To find out the significant difference in cooperative learning of higher secondary school students based on their wake up time during school days.
28. To find out the significant difference in achievement in Chemistry of higher secondary school students based on their wake up time during school days.
29. To find out the significant difference in cooperative learning of higher secondary school students based on their usage of mobile phones.
30. To find out the significant difference in achievement in Chemistry of higher secondary school students based on their usage of mobile phones.
31. To find out the significant difference in cooperative learning of higher secondary school students based on learning through tution.
32. To find out the significant difference in achievement in Chemistry of higher secondary school students based on learning through tution.
33. To find out the significant relationship between cooperative learning and achievement in Chemistry of higher secondary school students.

RESEARCH HYPOTHESES

1. The level of cooperative learning of higher secondary school students is moderate in nature.
2. The level of achievement in Chemistry of higher secondary school students is moderate in nature.
3. There is no significant difference in cooperative learning of higher secondary school students based on gender.
4. There is no significant difference in achievement in Chemistry of higher secondary school students based on gender.
5. There is no significant difference in cooperative learning of higher secondary school students based on type of management.
6. There is no significant difference in achievement in Chemistry of higher secondary school students based on type of management.

7. There is no significant difference in cooperative learning of higher secondary school students based on type of family.
8. There is no significant difference in achievement in Chemistry of higher secondary school students based on type of family.
9. There is no significant difference in cooperative learning of higher secondary school students based on medium of learning.
10. There is no significant difference in achievement in Chemistry of higher second ary school students based on medium of learning.
11. There is no significant difference in cooperative learning of higher secondary school students based on father's educational qualification.
12. There is no significant difference in achievement in Chemistry of higher secondary school students based father's educational qualification.
13. There is no significant difference in cooperative learning of higher secondary school students based on father's occupation.
14. There is no significant difference in achievement in Chemistry of higher secondary school students based on father's occupation.
15. There is no significant difference in cooperative learning of higher secondary school students based on mother's educational qualification.
16. There is no significant difference in achievement in Chemistry of higher secondary school students based on mother's educational qualification.
17. There is no significant difference in cooperative learning of higher secondary school students based on mother's occupation.
18. There is no significant difference in achievement in Chemistry of higher secondary school students based on mother's occupation.
19. There is no significant difference in cooperative learning of higher secondary school students based on their field of interest.
20. There is no significant difference in achievement in Chemistry of higher secondary school students based on their field of interest.
21. There is no significant difference in cooperative learning of higher secondary school students based on locality of house.
22. There is no significant difference in achievement in Chemistry of higher secondary school students based on locality of house.
23. There is no significant difference in cooperative learning of higher secondary school students based on the mode of transport.
24. There is no significant difference in achievement in Chemistry of higher secondary school students based on the mode of transport.
25. There is no significant difference in cooperative learning of higher secondary school students based on family monthly income.
26. There is no significant difference in achievement in Chemistry of higher secondary school students based on family monthly income.

27. There is no significant difference in cooperative learning of higher secondary school students based on their wake up time during school days.
28. There is no significant difference in achievement in Chemistry of higher secondary school students based on their wake up time during school days.
29. There is no significant difference in cooperative learning of higher secondary school students based on their usage of mobile phones.
30. There is no significant difference in achievement in Chemistry of higher secondary school students based on their usage of mobile phones.
31. There is no significant difference in cooperative learning of higher secondary school students based on learning through tuition.
32. There is no significant difference in achievement in Chemistry of higher secondary school students based on learning through tuition.
33. There is no significant relationship between cooperative learning and achievement in Chemistry of higher secondary school students.

SAMPLE OF THE STUDY

Data was collected from the higher secondary students adopting stratified random sampling method. The total sample size was 320 drawn from 6 schools were selected for the study belonging to different types of management: Government, Government Aided, Private schools in Vellore district, Tamil Nadu.

TOOLS AND TECHNIQUES USED

Researcher has used two important tools to identify the Cooperative learning and Achievement in Chemistry of higher secondary school students for that the following tools have been used.

Cooperative learning assessment scale by Researcher Kalpana .S and Arnold Robinson .D (2015)

Achievement in Chemistry assessment scale by Researcher Kalpana .S and Arnold Robinson .D (2015)

MAJOR FINDINGS OF THE STUDY

1. It was found that the level of cooperative learning among higher secondary school students is moderate in nature.
2. It was found that the level of achievement in Chemistry among higher secondary school students is moderate in nature.
3. It was found that there is significant difference in cooperative learning among higher secondary school students based on the gender.

4. Female students have significantly higher cooperative learning than male students.
5. It was found that there is significant difference in achievement in Chemistry among higher secondary school students based on the gender.
6. Female students have significantly higher achievement in Chemistry than male students.
7. It was found that there is significant difference in cooperative learning among higher secondary school students based on the type of management.
8. Student those who are studying in Government school have high cooperative learning than Government-Aided and Private higher secondary schools.
9. It was found that there is significant difference in achievement in Chemistry among higher secondary school students based on the type of management.
10. Student those who are studying in Government school have high achievement in Chemistry than Government-Aided and Private higher secondary schools.
11. It was found that there is significant difference in cooperative learning among higher secondary school students based on the type of family.
12. Nuclear family students have significantly higher cooperative learning than joint family students.
13. It was found that there is significant difference in Achievement in Chemistry among higher secondary school students based on the type of family.
14. Nuclear family students have significantly higher achievement in Chemistry than joint family students.
15. It was found that there is significant difference in cooperative learning among higher secondary school students based on the medium of learning.
16. Tamil medium students have significantly higher cooperative learning than English medium students.
17. It was found that there is significant difference in achievement in Chemistry among higher secondary school students based on the medium of learning.
18. Tamil medium students have significantly higher achievement in Chemistry than English medium students.
19. It was found that there is no significant difference in cooperative learning among higher secondary school students based on the father's educational qualification.

20. It was found that there is no significant difference in achievement in Chemistry among higher secondary school students based on the father's educational qualification.
21. It was found that there is no significant difference in cooperative learning among higher secondary school students based on the father's occupation.
22. It was found that there is no significant difference in achievement in Chemistry among higher secondary school students based on the father's occupation.
23. It was found that there is no significant difference in cooperative learning among higher secondary school students based on the mother's educational qualification.
24. It was found that there is no significant difference in achievement in Chemistry among higher secondary school students based on the mother's educational qualification.
25. It was found that there is no significant difference in cooperative learning among higher secondary school students based on the mother's occupation.
26. It was found that there is no significant difference in achievement in Chemistry among higher secondary school students based on the mother's occupation.
27. It was found that there is significant difference in cooperative learning among higher secondary school students based on their field of interest.
28. It was found that there is significant difference in achievement in Chemistry among higher secondary school students based on their field of interest.
29. It was found that there is no significant difference in cooperative learning among higher secondary school students based on locality of house.
30. It was found that there is no significant difference in achievement in Chemistry among higher secondary school students based on locality of house.
31. It was found that there is no significant difference in cooperative learning among higher secondary school students based on the mode of transport.
32. It was found that there is no significant difference in achievement in Chemistry among higher secondary school students based on the mode of transport.
33. It was found that there is no significant difference in cooperative learning among higher secondary school students based on family monthly income.

34. It was found that there is no significant difference in achievement in Chemistry among higher secondary school students based on family monthly income.
35. It was found that there is no significant difference in cooperative learning among higher secondary school students based on their wake up time during school days.
36. It was found that there is no significant difference in achievement in Chemistry among higher secondary school students based on their wake up time during school days.
37. It was found that there is no significant difference in cooperative learning among higher secondary school students based on their usage of mobile phones.
38. It was found that there is no significant difference in achievement in Chemistry among higher secondary school students based on their usage of mobile phones.
39. It was found that there is significant difference in cooperative learning among higher secondary school students based on learning through tuition.
40. Students who do not attend tuitions have significantly higher cooperative learning than those who attend tuition.
41. It was found that there is significant difference in achievement in Chemistry among higher secondary school students based on learning through tuition.
42. Students who do not attend tuitions have significantly higher achievement in Chemistry than those who attend tuition.
43. It was found that that there is significant and positive correlation on the cooperative learning and achievement in Chemistry among higher secondary school students.

EDUCATIONAL IMPLICATION

The results of this study provided strong support for the concept of the cooperative learning. It must be ensured that the group is aware of the objectives of the task and that they understand all relevant concepts. The teacher can set up the groups or allow the groups to decide their members themselves.

Here the level of cooperative learning and achievement in Chemistry of higher secondary school students is moderate, but it has to be increase to have higher level in achievement. So, it is important to keep the groups together, even when things are not going well with the group. The members of this group must learn to resolve problems, which is an essential part of collaborative learning. Teachers should give various methods of teaching related to student centred methodologies to increase their achievement.

From this study, researcher identified that female students have high cooperative learning and achievement in Chemistry. In the case of male students, the teachers must specify their responsibilities and possible consequences of failure to achieve in their studies. Teachers can give some reasonable suggestions for the male students to have high cooperative learning which produce high achievement.

Students studying in Government schools exhibit high cooperative learning and achievement in Chemistry Freedom to work, influence of peer group, Interest in the subject are the expected qualities of a school to have high achievement. Autonomy of the students such as deciding their own tasks and assigning the roles will depend on the skills and capabilities of the students. Students must be given time and activities to get to know each other before they have to begin working together and this plays a vital role for the well being of the project.

Students who studying in their vernacular (Tamil) medium have higher cooperative learning and achievement in Chemistry students express their views clearly and have high cooperation in studies at the time of usage of their mother tongue.

In this study cooperative learning and achievement in Chemistry have positive correlation, which indicates the change in the cooperative learning process cause the change in achievement in Chemistry. Educational institutions should help the learning to develop cooperative learning among students. Group study, project work, group project, exhibition, field visit are the few areas could be included in the curriculum is compulsory for the development of cooperative learning.

DELIMITATIONS

- The study had the following delimitations.
- The study has been restricted to Vellore District.
- The sample was restricted to 320 students.
- The study is confined to a sample of students chosen from Government/ Government Aided/ Private Schools.
- Only 11th standard students were chosen for the study.

SUGGESTION FOR THE FURTHER STUDY

After this study, researcher would like to suggest few topics for other researchers.

- The present study is confined to a representative sample of the students from the higher secondary school. It is therefore suggested that the similar studies can be done to Arts and Science College student.

- This study can be extended to other districts.
- Engineering students could also be included as sample of the study.
- The study can be under taken at the State and National level.

CONCLUSION

From this study researcher have come to a conclusion that cooperative learning and achievement in Chemistry had a positive relation which is essential for bright future. In educational institutions the students are motivated to develop their cooperative behaviour. Researcher has drawn many findings and few are shown in the educational implication. Through this study researcher has contributed many innovative solutions to enhance students learning. Suggestions for further study are also given to have continuity in research. On the whole this study gave a healthy way to overcome learning problem, by inculcating cooperative behaviour in their learning process. ❐

11

Problem and its Perspectives

Delinquency is defined as 'that behaviour in which members of a social group defy or violate their societal norms. This concept applies both to criminal acts of deviance and non criminal acts' (Hirsichi , 1969). Typical behaviour in delinquency includes: being a runway, shoplifting, drug abuse, liquor offences and assaults of varying degrees. From psychological perspective delinquency is termed as 'super ego deficiency' (Prinz 1997) whereas, behavioural perspective holds that the "overall level of childhood deviance is found to be an important predictor of adult deviance then anyone particular childhood behaviour (Sharma, 2012).

Families are major socializing agent for children and the foundation of human society. Children who are rejected by their parents, who grow up in homes with considerable conflict or who are inadequately supervised are at the greatest risk of becoming delinquent (Wright and Wright 1994). Family's influences in the early years of life of delinquents are intense. Parental ill mannerism, violence, alcohol abuse, maladaptive upbringing and poor living conditions are important determinant of criminal behavior.

Children having fewer possibilities to legally satisfy their needs often select inappropriate ways to satisfy their needs.

Self Confidence is an individual's sense of his or her value or worth that is the extent to which a person values, approves of, appreciates, prizes or likes himself/herself (Blascovich & Tomaka 1991). It reflects a person's overall evaluation or appraisal of his or her worth.

STATEMENT OF THE PROBLEM

The present study has been entitled as "Family Environment and Self Confidence among IX Standard Students".

OPERATIONAL DEFINITION

According to the view of the investigator "Family Environment" is measured by the total scores obtained in the Family Environment Scale prepared and validated by Harpreet Bhatia and Chandha. N.K. (1993)

DEFINITION OF FAMILY

According to Maclver and Page, (1956), "Family is the most important primary group in the society. The family is a group defined by a close relationship sufficiently precise and endearing to provide for the production and upbringing of children".

According to Kingsley Davis, (1966), "Family is a group of persons whose relations to one another are based upon consanguinity and who are therefore kin to one another".

According to Oxford Dictionary of Sociology, "The Family is an intimate domestic group made up of people related to one another by bonds of blood or legalities. It has been a very resilient social unit that has survived and adopted though time".

According to Ogburn and Ninkoff (1952), "Family is more or less durable association of husband and wife with or without children, or of Man or Women along with children."

THE CONCEPT OF FAMILY

The Family is the basic primary group and the natural matrix of personality Broadly speaking, the family is a single unit of people who live together, share life's basic day-today functions. Human beings demonstrate the need for such a core group and the need for each individual to grow.

FEATURES OF FAMILY

- The Family is basic, definite and enduring group.
- Family is formed by the relatively durable companionship of husband and wife, and their relationship.
- The family includes the couples and theft children; the family procreated and brings up children.
- Family can be large in size in which people of several generations stay together.

- The family consists of only the husband, wife or only the father and this children or only the mother or her children.
- When many generations of people live together it is a joint of family.

FUNCTIONS OF FAMILY

Broadly speaking, functions of the family may be divided into two

- Essential functions
- Non - essential functions.

Basic functions of family include bringing up of children, division of labor and group satisfaction. Reproduction of children and providing them food, clothing and shelter are some essential functions of the family. Taking Care of children's health, betterment of economic conditions and providing them recreation are some of the subsidiary function of family. In addition to the above mentioned essential functions, a family has many non-essential functions as well. Some of the non-essential functions are explained below.

ECONOMIC FUNCTIONS

In the economic field it is the responsibility of the family to see that there is proper division of work. It is the function of the family to see that the economic needs of the people are met and all members get minimum money which is necessary for meeting their needs.

SOCIAL FUNCTIONS

Family is required to perform social functions. It is the centre of all social activities. An individual gets his social status through the family. A family helps its members through which they can move socially forward.

CULTURAL FUNCTIONS

Family is the centre of all cultural activities. It sees that its members are molded according to family culture and that is how the cultural heritage is preserved. We find that what a family member is taught in his childhood is preserved throughout his life. Members of the family are made to live up to cultural heritage of the family.

EDUCATIONAL FUNCTIONS

It is the responsibility of every family that it should teach the children and give them good education. It should see that none is illiterate. In fact family is one of the most important educational agencies. The child gets the first lesson only in the family. In addition to several indications, a family provides and arranges for vocational education of its members as well.

DIFFERENT FAMILY RELATIONS

Basis from large families in which the children are closely spaced, have fewer direct contact with mothers who are preoccupied with other responsibilities. As a result they suffer from some of the usual effects of maternal deprivation not only lack of opportunities for emotional attachment but also lack of maternal attention and stimulation. Lack of attention and stimulation can often cause them to become lethargic and to do less than their capacity.

PARENT CHILD RELATIONS

The care and socialization of children are the most important social tasks that are entrusted to the family. Parents raising their children in a climate of affection and responsiveness, using clear and explicable rules, providing developmentally enhancing and autonomous environments, are more likely to have children with a positive self-concept; they are emotionally stable, socially competent, well accepted by their peers, academically successful and intrinsically self-responsible.

It has been argued that in contrast to the west, the value system of the Eastern World is quite different, centering more on sociability, calmness and passive contemplation; accordingly, parental, socialization practices have been shown to differ markedly from western standards to ensure an appropriate transmission of these values.

SIBLING RELATIONS

Despite declining birth rate in the industrialized countries, the sibling relationship still contributes substantially to the process of individual and family development. Beside the more structural properties of sibling constellations and their impact on intra and extra familiar relationships, more fine grained behavioural analyses have show that differential parental treatment is strongly related to the quality of sibling relationships. Siblings who are treated differently by their parents tend to develop poorer and more conflict relationships among themselves and show more adaptation problems as adolescents.

Although siblings tend to develop a closer and less competitive relationship in later life, much more knowledge is required about differential developmental paths of sibling relationship in a lifespan perspective.

HAZARDS OF FAMILY RELATIONSHIP

Friction with family members has two serious effects; it weakens family ties and it leads to a habitual unfavourable pattern of adjustment to people and problems which is carried outside the home.

- Separation from family
- Failure to develop attachment behaviour

- Deterioration in family relationship
- Over protectiveness
- Inconsistent training
- Child abuse

EFFECTS OF ATTITUDE OF FAMILY RELATIONSHIP

The attitudes of different family members, the foundation of which have generally been laid before a child is born, have a profound influence not only on the child but also on family relationship. This influence may be favourable or unfavourable, depending not on attitude of one family member but on the attitude of all the family members.

OPERATIONAL DEFINITION

According to the view of the investigator the term "Self confidence" refers to the overall score obtained by the IX standard students on the Personality Type Assessment Questionnaire constructed by Suresh Kumar.M and Vaiyapuri Raja.V (2010).

DEFINITION OF CONFIDENCE

Confidence is generally described as a state of being certain either that a hypothesis or prediction is correct or that a chosen course of action is the best or most effective. Self-confidence is having confidence in oneself. Arrogance or hubris in this comparison, is having unmerited confidence - believing something or someone is capable or correct when they are not. Overconfidence or presumptuousness is excessive belief in someone (or something) succeeding, without any regard for failure. Confidence can be a self-flitting prophecy as those without it may fail or not try because they lack it and those with it may succeed because they have it rather than because of an innate ability.

SELF CONFIDENCE

Self-confidence does not necessarily imply 'self-belief' or a belief in one's ability to succeed. For instance, one may be inept at a particular sport or activity, but remain 'confident' in one's demeanour, simply because one does not place a great deal or emphasis on the outcome of the activity. When one does not dwell on negative consequences one can be more 'self-confident' because one is worrying far less about failure or the disapproval of others following potential failure. One is then more likely to focus on the actual situation which means that enjoyment and success in that situation is also more probable. Belief in one's abilities to perform an activity comes through successful experience and may add to, or consolidate, a general sense of self-confidence. Studies have also found a link between high levels of confidence and wages. Seemingly, those who self-report they were confident earlier in schooling, earned better wages and were promoted more quickly over the life course.

FACTORS AFFECTING SELF- CONFIDENCE

Self-esteem has been directly connected to an individual's social network, the activities they participate in, and what they hear about themselves from others. Positive self-esteem has been linked to factors such as psychological health, mattering to others, and both body image and physical health. On the contrary, low self-esteem has been associated with the outcomes of depression, health problems, and antisocial behavior. Usually, adolescents of poor health will display low self-esteem. Globally, self-confidence in boys and girls will decline during adolescence, and in contrast to boys, girls' self-confidence won't shoot back up again until early adulthood.

During adolescence, self-esteem is affected by age, race, ethnicity, puberty, health, body height, body weight, body image, involvement in physical activities, gender presentation, gender identity, and awakening or discovery of sexuality. Self-confidence can vary and be observed in a variety of dimensions. Components of one's social and academic life affect self-esteem. An individual's self-confidence can vary in different environments, such as at home or in school.

IMPLICIT VS EXPLICIT SELF CONFIDENCE

Implicit can be defined as something that is implied or understood though not directly expressed. Explicit is defined as something that is fully and clearly expressed; leaving nothing implied. Implicitly measured self-esteem has been found to be weakly correlated with explicitly measured self-esteem. This leads some critics to assume that explicit and implicit self-confidence are two completely different types of self-esteem. Therefore, this has drawn the conclusion that one will either have a distinct, unconscious self-esteem or they will consciously misrepresent how they feel about themselves. Recent studies have shown that implicit self-esteem doesn't particularly tap into your unconscious, rather that people consciously over report levels of self-esteem. Another possibility is that implicit measurement may be assessing a different aspect of conscious self-esteem altogether. Inaccurate self-evaluation is commonly observed in healthy populations. In the extreme, large differences between one's self-perception and one's actual behavior is a hallmark of a number of disorders that have important implications for understanding treatment seeking and compliance.

People who struggle with self-esteem are often advised to seek out people who are successful, confident and have high self-esteem. Of course it's not as simple to just watch someone who is outwardly comfortable and hope that will rub off and improve the self-esteem. It wills not, if this self esteem requires improving has to be made. However, it is useful to spend some time with people with high self-esteem and observe some of the specific characteristic that are common with people who are confident and 'comfortable in own skin'. Listed below are 7 common traits.

1. **Belief in Themselves:** People who have high self-esteem have confidence in own abilities. This isn't a case of false self-confidence. They recognize what they're good at, are confident that they are able to improve where necessary and unlike people with low self-esteem, believe that they deserve to do better. The effect of this is that they are often ambitious in chosen field and do well in careers as they consistently strive for improvement and personal success. They don't waste time indulging in negative self-work.
2. **Know what they want or Need:** People with high self-esteem generally have clear ideas about what they want or need and are able to communicate these needs and wants to others.
3. **Effective Communication Skills:** It's common for people with high self-esteem to be good communicators. This includes having good listening skills which leave them open to taking advice, being open to change and new ideas.
4. **Drive to Succeed:** Not surprisingly people with high self-esteem have the drive to succeed. Some people with low self-esteem have similar drive, but the difference is that people with high self-esteem are generally more flexible and find it easier to overcome challenges and disappointments along the way. They don't worry about failure and even when they do fail, they have the inner resources to learn from the failure and then move on.
5. **Comfortable with Change:** Because people with high self-esteem are comfortable with change, they enthusiastically seek out new opportunities and are open to embracing new ideas. They are also happy to learn new skills to support them with any new challenges.
6. **Enjoy Healthy Relationships:** With good communication skills and enthusiasm to succeed, people with high self-esteem generally enjoy good healthy relationship and are able to accept constructive criticism, without letting it dent confidence. Because of confidence they are rarely competitive with others because they are comfortable with own abilities.
7. **Goal - Orientated:** The almost inbred confidence that someone with high self-esteem has, means that they are very focused on self-improvement and success and are often good at planning and setting goals in a methodical way, as well as achieving them.

If we have low self-esteem it's easy to envy those people who exude confidence and have high self-esteem. Probably the best thing that you can learn from people who have high self-esteem is that they are comfortable with change and are prepared to have a go. That may sound overly simpbstic but if you're struggling with low self-esteem it's only that individual who can make the commitment to change, reduce the negative and take a risk.

PERSONALITY OF A CONFIDENT PERSON

1. **Self - Assured** - Confident people believe in themselves, and they believe that life fulfills a special purpose in the world. They know strengths and have accepted weakness.
2. **Ambitious** - Confident people know what they want. They easily define goals and strive to achieve them. This could be most significant trait of a confident person.
3. **Sociable** - They are adept at navigating various social situations with seeming ease. This ease is borne of the belief that they belong in any environment. Confident people know how to endear themselves to others and how to take compliments and criticisms gracefully.
4. **Competitive** - Confident people love competition; they love to test mettle against the best efforts of others, because they believe they can win, even when they lose.
5. **Risk Taking** - They take risks because they are not afraid to lose, or to be wrong. While they are confident in abilities, they also know instinctively that nobody wins them all, and that they will likely win out the next time.
6. **Hard Working** - Confident people know the best path to achieving goals is through putting in hard effort, to matter how exhaustive or Hard - working people are confident, and confident people are hard - working. It's a chicken - egg thing.
7. **Determined** -They also never give up on goals, even when it sometimes seems impossible. They know that it is better to try and fail and try again than to give up and let doubt take over.
8. **Accepting** - Confident people are often the most accepting people, taking others so they come, no matter short comings. They succeed at this because most confident people have recognized own short comings and realize that the path forward is not about keeping other people down.
9. **Shrewd** - Often, awareness and cleverness breed confidence. Confident people are often good at quickly sizing up other people and figuring out social hierarchies and situations.

10. **Positive -** Confident people are simply put, positive people. They know how to assuage doubts, conquer fears, and how to find every silver lining in a sky gone gray with storm clouds. They know that white failure is a part of everyday life, even in failure fresh starts are always possible.

NEED FOR THE STUDY

The Family Environment is one of the most important factors that gives the child a firsthand experience of living and learning. It is in the home, that the children feels secure, happy and a warm atmosphere that makes the children very close and intimate with the parents.

Personality and Self Confidence is significance in today's world. It may be define as one's ability to know, feel, judge, behave, adopt to the environment, co-operate with a person's behavioral a proper way with the ultimate realization of happiness in him/her. In view of its wide significance from the individuals as well as it becomes quite imperative that serious efforts should be made for its proper development right from early childhood among human being. Family Environment and Self Confident are important for survival, decision making, boundary setting, communication and making unity in the society which are essential to makes one's life happy.

OBJECTIVES OF THE STUDY

The following objectives are set in the present study.

1. To find out the level of Family Environment of IX standard students.
2. To find out the level of Self Confidence of IX standard students.
3. To find out the significant difference in the Family Environment of IX standard students based on Gender.
4. To find out the significant difference in the Family Environment of IX standard students based on Type of School
5. To find out the significant difference in the Family Environment of IX standard students based on Type of Management.
6. To find out the significant difference in the Family Environment of IX standard students based on Father's Qualification
7. To find out the significant difference in the Family Environment of IX standard students based on Father's Occupation.
8. To find out the significant difference in the Family Environment of IX standard students based on Mother's Qualification.
9. To find out the significant difference in the Family Environment of IX standard students based on Mother's Occupation.

10. To find out the significant difference in the Family Environment of IX standard students based on Type of Family.
11. To find out the significant difference in the Self Confidence of IX standard students based on Gender
12. To find out the significant difference in the Self Confidence of IX standard students based on Type of School
13. To find out the significant difference in the Self Confidence of IX standard students based on Type of Management.
14. To find out the significant difference in the Self Confidence of IX standard students based on Father's Qualification
15. To find out the significant difference in the Self Confidence of IX standard students based on Father's Occupation.
16. To find out the significant difference in the Self Confidence of IX standard students based on Mother's Qualification.
17. To find out the significant difference in the Self Confidence of IX standard students based on Mother's Occupation.
18. To find out the significant difference in the Self Confidence of IX standard students based on Type of Family.

DELIMITATIONS OF THE STUDY

The present study had the following delimitation

- Only high school students were chosen for investigation.
- The sample has been chosen from Trichy District.
- The sample is confined into 300, due to lack of time.

CONCLUSION

The first chapter is chiefly concerned with the conceptual framework of the problem chosen for the study. The discussion on Family Environment and Self Confidence is dealt in detain in the present chapter. The different aspects and areas of the study is highlighted in this chapter.

❐

12

Review of Related Literature

For any worthwhile study in any field of knowledge the research worker needs an adequate familiarity with the work which has already been done in the area of their choice. In review of related studies the researcher attempts to determine what others have learnt about similar research problems and to gather information relevant to the research problem at hand.

The reviews of related literature serve multiple purposes and are essential to a well designed research study.

PURPOSE OF REVIEW OF RELATED LITERATURE

The major purpose of reviewing the literature is to determine what has already been done that related to our topic. This knowledge not only avoids unintentional duplication, but it also provides the understandings and insights necessary to develop a logical frame work into which out topic fits. In other works, the review tells the researcher what has been done and in so doing, also suggests what needs to be done. Earlier studies can provide the rationale for our research hypothesis; and indications of what needs to be done often form the basis for justifying the significance of our study.

Another important function of the literature review is to point out research strategies and specific procedures and measuring instruments that have and have not been found to be productive investing out topic. This information will help us to avoid researcher's mistakes and to profit from their experiences.

STUDIES RELATED TO FAMILY ENVIRONMENT

Foreign Studies Related to Family Environment

Brown, JD (1999), conducted an elaborate study to find out the relationship, between the dimensions of Self Concept and Family relationship. It was proved from this study that racial and ethnic difference with family relationship greatly affected the academic achievement of the students.

Vaughn, DA (2000), analysed the students with learning disabilities with respect to their family relationship. Various factories responsible for learning disabilities were analyzed and the result given has shown that family relationship influenced the learning disabilities of the students.

Burke, ME (2002), made an effort to study the school student's perception of family relationship in relation to their Self Concept, attitude and achievement. The main objectives of the study were to find out the significant association between family relationship of the students and the variables Self Concept, attitude and achievement. This study reveals the fact those family relationship inferences the Self Concept of the individual.

Ryan, Brace (2002), studied the importance of family relationship on the academic achievement of the children. This study, conducted in Canada aimed at studying the academic achievement of school children. This study has conducted that the students having good relationship with their family members got motivation from their parents and should have good academic achievement.

Mokrun K, (2003), conducted a study among the school children to find out the role of family environment in social competence. This study which was conducted among the urban school children used social and emotional skills curricular to find out the role of family in the development of social competence among the school children.

Wehrman, Kathleen Gonzalez, (2003), analyzed in a study, the influence of family variables on the development of personality of the children. This study showed that family variables make a difference in the personality of the students. Children with good socio economic status were found to be having good personality than those who come from poor socio economic conditions.

Bradley, Kathleen, (2004), investigated the role of school, family and individual factors in the academic success of school students at three achievement level and of special education students with mild disabilities. The major aim of this study was to find out the significant difference between the normal and the disabled children with respect to various family factors.

Wilson, S.S, (2004), studied the validation of the identity development inventory with dysfunctional families. This study revealed the fact that the students with good family relationship were able to identify their abilities.

Michaci, Shannon, (2007), studied the family and community involvement in schools; results from the school health policies and programs study 2006. Family and community involvement in schools linked strongly to improved in the academic achievements of students, better school attendance, and improved school programs and quality.

Martinz – Gonzalz, (2008), investigated the family involvement in the education of potential drop – out children. This paper focuses on family involvement in the education of teenagers at risk of dropping out from compulsory secondary school. A questionnaire was completed by 131 spacing and Cypriot families with children at six schools.

Indian Studies Related to Family Environment

Dogra, Anupama, (2004), conducted a study about the infrastructural facilities, parental attitudes, home conditions, and socio economic back ground in relation to educational aspiration of higher secondary school students. The finding of the study has proved that, students, with good home conditions and socio-economic background had very good educational aspiration.

Ramesh Rani, (2004), investigated the contribution of home, class room and educational environment in relation to achievement in political science at the senior secondary school level. One of the major objectives of this study was to find out the association between the family variables and the achievement of the students. This study had affirmed the fact that family environment certainly influenced the educational aspiration of the students.

Arun Christopher T, (2006), investigated the influence of family Relationship on the Achievement in physics among Higher Secondary School students. This conducted in Dharmapuri District of Tamil Nadu had proved that the students with good family environment were able to get good performance.

Bini, (2006), conducted a study on family environment and academic achievement among higher secondary school students in Dharmapuri District of Tamil Nadu. In the study she attempted to find out the level of Family Environment and educational aspiration of the students and the association between there variables. The findings have proved that family environment variables influenced the educational aspiration of students.

STUDIES RELATED TO SELF CONFIDENCE

Foreign Studies Related to Self Confidence

Clement and Richard, (1994), studied the social psychological constructs to examine the linguistic attitude and motivations of 301 Hungarian high school students learning English as a foreign Language (EFL). Factor and correlation analyses of the results of a survey questionnaire revealed that xenophile, socio-cultural, Instrumental, and media-use reasons were most strongly endorsed by the students.

Archeries et al., (1999), studied on coping at university. An Examination of Achievement, Motivation, Self Regulation, Confidence, and Method of Entry. Studied the interrelationships among characteristics of undergraduate students and the characteristics that predicted achievement in sample of 71 mature-age students entering from an enabling program and 61 younger students entering from high school. Results add to the literature on links between psychological characteristics and academic achievement and show that these mature- age students are coping at least as well as their younger counterparts.

Green, Reed, (2000), investigated the social context differences in relation of self esteem and self confidence during late adolescence. In a study of 39 college and 43 non-college youths, social context significantly differentiated self confidence and self esteem college youth were higher in self esteem adjustment and achievement.

Rogat, Marcia, (2005), described Kid-to-Kid, a group discussion program that gives students a strong voice and kits them connect with their peers in an environment where it as safe to be honest, where feelings and thoughts can be expressed without fear of judgment, and where the teacher talks less than the students. Guidelines for starting such a program are presented. In facilitating such classroom discussions, teachers can convey trust in their students ability to reason, their desire for fairness, and their capacity for wisdom.

Jennings and Janelle Perron, (2009), found that there are three conclusions that can be drawn from this study. First, affected participant Self Confidence varying degrees for a majority of women in the sample. Second, first year women experienced more leadership related change as a result of their participation than second year peers. Third, the program is not reaching emerging leaders exclusively because of the high rate of involvement that any of the women in the sample possessed upon entering the program.

Indian Studies Related to Self Confidence

Dipika, Shah and Manivannan, (2003), studied the self confidence of visually impaired children in integrated and special schools in Tamil Nadu. A sample of 320 visually impaired children was selected the sample through stratified random sampling procedure. The tools used students Self Confidence scale (SCS) based on the Liker scale of summate ratings. Major findings of the study were 1. There was no significant difference between the scores of visually impaired children in Self Confidence on the basis of the gender. 2. There was no significant interaction between independent variables gender and nature of impairment as far as the scores of visually impaired children in Self

Confidence are concerned is tenable. 3. There was no significant interaction between independent variables gender and nature of schools as far as the scores of visually impaired children in Self Confidence are concerned.

Subramaniam, Leena Mathew, (2004), studied assessing Self Confidence, mental health & frustration among injured sportsmen & women. The sample comprised 60 of which 30 were sportsmen and used to the other assess Self Confidence 30 were sports women. Rekha Agnihotri's tool was Tovier personality inventory (TPI) was used to assess frustration. Major findings of the study were. 1. There were significant differences in the Self Confidence and frustration between injured sportsmen and sportswomen. 2. There was no significant difference in mental health, Self Confidence and frustration, and mental health and frustration of both.

Geeta, Pasteyand Vijayalaxmi, Aminbhavi, (2006), studied the Impact in emotional maturity on stress and Self Confidence of adolescents. Sample of the study consists of105 adolescents studying in XI and XII class at Dharwad city Karnataka state, India. The scales such as emotional maturity (Singh and Bhargav, 1994), Self Confidence inventory (Rekha Agnihotri, 1987) and student's stress scale (Deo, 1997) were administrated on the selected sample. The findings revealed that the adolescents with high emotional maturity have significantly high stress ($t=10,44; p<0.001$) and Self Confidence ($t=2.92; <0.01$) when compared to those with low emotional maturity.

Tirath Singh and Parminder Kaur, (2008), studied the effect of meditation on Self Confidence of student teacher in relation to gender and religion. Sample of the study were used 152 student teacher of B.Ed. the tools were used Self Confidence inventory (1987) in Hindi developed by the Dr.Rekha Agnihotry,and Raven's standard progressive matrices developed by J. Raven, J.C. Raven and J.H. Court (revised 2000) were used. Major findings of the study were 1.there was significant effect of gender on Self Confidence when pre-Self Confidence was taken as a covariate 2. There was no significant effect of interaction between meditation and gender on Self Confidence when Pre-Self Confidence was taken as a covariate. 3. There was no significant effect of iteration meditation and gender on Self Confidence when Pre-Self Confidence and Pre-general intelligence were taken as covariates.

Ali Haydarsar, Ramazan Aveu Abdullah Isiklar, (2010), studied the under graduate student's self-confidence levels in terms of some variables. Self- confidence has a very significant impact both on expressing yourself during interpersonal relations and making up relations with others. Acting without self-confidence may lead to isolation or retreatment of an individual from society. Because of that, therapists have been very much concerned about self-confidence. Many people have difficulty in asserting rights. These people should increase self-confidence levels in proper situations. In this context, self-confidence education consists of modeling people who are self confident, acting to show that you are self-confident enough and reacting instantly. This research was made in order to analyze undergraduate students' self-confidence levels in terms of some variables. The population of the study consisted of four departments at Aksaray University. As a sample, 168 students studying at Aksaray University took part in. Data were collected via a scale measuring self-confidence levels of students. In data analyses, descriptive analyses, t-test and ANOVA were used. Results of the study showed that there was significant difference in terms of gender and departments.

Parvathamma and Sharanamma, (2010), studied the anxiety level and level of Self Confidence and relation with academic achievement six high schools of Chamrajnagar taluk in karanataka were selected randomly. Totally 300 students were selected by randomly selecting 5 students from each school including boys and girls. Tools were used Self Confidence checklist (M.Basavanna), anxiety scale (Prof D.N.Srivastasva &Dr.Govind Tiwari), school records for academic achievement, major findings of the study were : 1. There was a significant difference between anxiety level of boys and girls. 2. There was a significant difference between Self Confidence level of boys and girls.

Sabira Kleitman, Jennifar Gibsun, (2011), studied the Meta cognitive beliefs, self-confidence and primary learning environment of six grade students. Metacognition is an integral component of a self- regulated approach of learning. The present study examined the relationships between academic self-efficacy and perceptions of one's own competence in memory and reasoning abilities, and role in predicting the self-confidence trait. The study also aimed to determine the role of key classroom factors(goal orientation and self-efficacy with the teacher) in predicting self-beliefs, the self-confidence trait and academic achievement in Year 6 students (N=177)EFA and path analysis were used to determine these relationships. The hypothesized path model was tested in a simultaneous fashion of the entire system of variables to determine whether or not hypothesized relationships were consistent with data. The result suggests that accede mica self-efficacy and Meta cognitive competency belief define a broad factor –Meta cognitive beliefs- which serves as a key predictor of self-confidence. Mastery goal-orientation and self efficacy with teacher predicted Meta cognitive beliefs and indirectly, self-confidence. Students with stronger Meta cognitive beliefs were less engaged in self-handicapping behaviours. Known common factors-intelligence, gender and a proxy for self-efficacy scale, school fees-were controlled for the present study has important implications for both Meta cognitive theory and educational practice.

CONCLUSION

The study of related literature has helped the investigator to have a clear perspective of the problem chosen for the present investigation. Keeping abreast of the work done in this field, the researcher has formulated the hypotheses for the present study. Designing the method of research, description of the variables, sample selection, selection of suitable tools, administration and scoring methods of responses have been undertaken based on the review which is discussed in the succeeding chapter.

❐

13

Research Design and Methodology

In the modern society research has become an important activity for its very progress. Research products new knowledge which takes the society forward. It enables to find solutions to problems and resolve conflicts in the society.

Research has been defined as, "A studious inquiry or Examination; especially critical and exhaustive investigation or experimental having for its aim the discovery of facts and their correct interpretation, the revision of accepted conclusions, theories or laws in the light of newly discovered facts or partial applications of new or revised conclusions, theories or laws"(Webster, 1981).

Develop new scientific tools, concepts and theories which would facilitate reliable and valid study of human behavior in decision making. (Aggarvan and Diwan, 1997).

The research process can be "Viewed as the overall scheme of scientific activities in which scientists engage in order to produce knowledge; it is paradigm to scientific inquiry" (Frankfort – Nachmias & nachmmias, 1992). Scientific activities satisfy the criteria of logical verification. The knowledge produced thus is provable both through reason experience or observation.

Research design is a catalogue of the various phases and facts relating to the formation of a research effort. It is arrangements of the essential conditions for collection and analysis of data in a term that aims to combine relevance to research propose with economy in the procedure.

This chapter deals with the research design and methodology used in the present study. It describes the operational definitions of key terms, hypotheses to be tested, population and sample of the study; tools used validity and reliability of the tools and statistical techniques used.

DESIGN OF THE STUDY

Choosing a design for a study basically involves selecting the most appropriate technique to solve the particular problem under investigation Anderson, Durson and Poole, (1970).

METHOD OF THE STUDY

The investigator adopts the survey method of research. In the words of Adi Seshaiah and Sulochanasekhar (1997). The survey method is necessary for the collection of facts and information relevant to the problem investigated. The survey approach to educational problems is one of the most commonly used approaches. It goes beyond mere gathering and tabulation of data, it involves interpretation, comparison, measurement classification, evaluation and generalization, all directed towards a proper understanding and solution of significant education problems. It brings info focus the existing educational problem and also suggests ways of meeting them.

HYPOTHESES OF THE STUDY

The hypotheses formed in the present study are listed below:

1. To find out the level of Family Environment of IX standard students.
2. To find out the level of Self- Confidence of IX standard students.
3. To find out the significant difference in the Family Environment of IX standard students based on Gender.
4. To find out the significant difference in the Family Environment of IX standard students based on Type of School
5. To find out the significant difference in the Family Environment of IX standard students based on Type of Management.
6. To find out the significant difference in the Family Environment of IX standard students based on Father's Qualification
7. To find out the significant difference in the Family Environment of IX standard students based on Father's Occupation.
8. To find out the significant difference in the Family Environment of IX standard students based on Mother's Qualification.

9. To find out the significant difference in the Family Environment of IX standard students based on Mother's Occupation.
10. To find out the significant difference in the Family Environment of IX standard students based on Type of Family.
11. To find out the significant difference in the Self Confidence of IX standard students based on Gender
12. To find out the significant difference in the Self Confidence of IX standard students based on Type of School
13. To find out the significant difference in the Self Confidence of IX standard students based on Type of Management.
14. To find out the significant difference in the Self Confidence of IX standard students based on Father's Qualification
15. To find out the significant difference in the Self Confidence of IX standard students based on Father's Occupation.
16. To find out the significant difference in the Self Confidence of IX standard students based on Mother's Qualification.
17. To find out the significant difference in the Self Confidence of IX standard students based on Mother's Occupation.
18. To find out the significant difference in the Self Confidence of IX standard students based on Type of Family.
19. To find out the significant difference in there is correlation between Family Environment and Self Confidence.

TOOLS USED FOR THE PRESENT STUDY

At the present, the investigator has selected the following tools to verify the hypotheses.

1. Family Environment Scale (FES) by Harrpreet Bhatia and Chadha N.K (1993).
2. Self Confidence Assessment Scale (SCAS) constructed and validated by Suresh Kumar. M and Vaiyauri Raja. M (2010).

DESCRIPTION ADMINISTRATION AND SCORING PROCEDURE OF THE TOOLS USED IN THE PRESENT STUDY

FAMILY ENVIRONMENT ASSESSMENT SCALE (FEAS)

Description of the Tool

This scale is constructed and validated by Dr.Harrpreet Bhatia and Dr.N.K.Chandha. This scale consists of 69 items with the response category of strongly agree, agree, neutral, disagree, and strongly disagree. This scale is having positive and negative items which are shown in the following table.

TABLE. 13.1: List of Postive and Negative Items

Item Types	Items	TotalItems
Positive	14,5,7,8,9,10,11,13,14,16,19,21,22,24,25,27,28,36,37,38,39,42,43,44,46,47,48,51,52,54,55,56,59,60,61,62,63,66,67,69	41
Negative	2,3,6,12,15,17,18,20,23,26,29,13,31,32,33,34,35,40,41,45,49,50,53,57,58,64,65,68	28
	Total	**69**

Administration of the Tool

From the instructions have been given to the students which are given below.

1. The purpose of the questionnaire is to know and to understand your view on Family Environment.
2. Please mark all items.
3. Information collected will be kept confidential.
4. Read each questions carefully and given suitable response by putting () Mark.

Scoring Procedure

This items were scored by the students response, the procedure is given in the table.

TABLE. 13.2: Showing the Scoring Procedure

Response	Positive Items	Negative Items
Strongly Agree	5	1
Agree	4	2
Neutral	3	3
Disagree	2	4
Strongly Disagree	1	5

SELF CONFIDENCE ASSESSMENT SCALE (SCAS)

Description of the tool

Self Confidence Assessment Scale was constructed and validated by Suresh Kumar. M and Vaiyauri Raja. M (2010). Respond educational ad psychological Research Center, Madurai. This Assessment Scale consists of 20 items in which 10 of them are negative items.

TABLE. 13.3: List of Positive and Negative Items

Positive (10)	1,2,3,4,5,6,7,8,9,10
Negative (10)	11,12,13,14,15,16,17,18,19,20

Administration of the tool

The IX Standard Students were instructed that the consists of 20 questions concerning Self Confidence. After each question there were three column "Agree" "No Idea" "Disagree". If they agreed with the question, they had to put a tick in the "Agree" column and If they disagreed with the question, they had to put a tick in the "Disagree" column. If they undecided they had put mark in the "No Idea". They were asked to answer all the questions.

Scoring Procedure

The scoring to the response given by the respondent should be like the following

TABLE. 13.4: Showing the Scoring Procedure

Response	Positive	Negative
Agree	2	0
Undecided	1	1
Disagree	0	2

PILOT STUDY

A pilot study was conducted to determine the suitability of the tool used in the present investigation. A random sample of 50 students was selected for the study to establish the reliability and the validity of the tools.

ESTABILISHING RELIABILITY

The reliability or a test may be defined as the degree of consistency with which the test measures what it does measures. A test score is called reliable, when we have a reason to believe it to be stable and trustworthy.

The reliability of the tools used for present study was established as follows.

Family Environmental Scale

To compute the reliability of Family Environment Scale, The split half method was employed, the reliability was computed and it was found to be 0.78 using Spearman Brown Formula.

Self Confidence

In order to establish the reliability of the Self Confidence, the split half method was used. The reliability of the Self Confidence scale was found to be 0.758.ESTABLISHING VALIDITY OF TOOLS

Family Environment Scale

The validity of Family Environment Scale was found out by computing the square root of the reliability coefficient which worked out to be 0.88.

Self Confidence

In the present study the validity coefficient is computed as the square root of the reliability coefficient and this works out to be 0.870 indicating that self confidence scale is valid questionnaire.

Main Study

The validated tools were made us for the main study to collect the necessary data. The study was carried out in 3 schools in the Family Environment and Self Confidence of High School Students.

SAMPLE OF THE STUDY

Data was collected from the high school students adopting stratified random sampling method. The total sample size was 300 drawn 3 schools were selected for the study belonging to different types of Management of schools: Government, Government Aided and Private schools. The details of school visited and number of students tested for investigation are given below.

The details of the sample selected from different types of school in Trichy District are given below.

TABLE. 13.5: Showing the Details of Sample Selected

S.No	Types of Management of Schools	Name of the school	Male	Female	Total
1.	Government School	A.D.W.S Higher Secondary School, Melagupparai.	50	50	100
2.	Government Aided School	Zamindar Higher Secondary School, Thuraiyur.	50	50	100
3.	Private School	Sowdambica Matriculation Higher Secondary School, Thuraiyur.	50	50	100
	Total		**150**	**150**	**300**

STATISTICAL TECHNIQUES USED

The following statistical techniques were used in the present study:

1. Descriptive analysis
2. Different analysis (F – ratio and Critical Ratio)
3. Correlation analysis (r)

i. MEAN

$$\text{SED}\left(\bar{X}\right) = A + \frac{\sum fd}{\sum f} \times i$$

Where,

A = Assumed mean

f = frequency

d = deviation from the assumed mean

i = Class interval

ii. STANDARD DEVIATION

$$\text{Standard Deviation,SD } (\sigma) = \sqrt{\frac{\sum fd^2}{N} - \left[\frac{\sum fd}{N}\right]^2} \times i$$

Where,

f = Frequency

d = Deviation from the assumed mean

I = Class interval

N = Total frequency

iii. 't' TEST

To continue the significance of difference between means of various measures test is used: 't' ratio is calculated from the relation.

$$\text{t-ratio} = \frac{M_1 \sim M_2}{\sqrt{\frac{\sigma_1^2}{N_1} + \frac{\sigma_1^2}{N_2}}} = \frac{M_1 \sim M_2}{S \in D}$$

Where,

$M_1\ M_2$ = Means of the groups

SED = Standard Error Deviation

iv. 'F'-TEST

F- ratio = Variance between the group/Variance within the group Correction term 'C'

$$C = \frac{\sum x_1 + \sum x_2 + \sum x_3}{N}$$

$$BSS = \left(\sum x_1\right)^2 / W_1 + \left(\sum x_2\right)^2 / W_2 + \left(\sum x_3\right)^2 W_3 - C$$

$$TSS = \sum x_1^2 + \sum x_2^2 + \sum x_3^2 - C$$

WSS= TSS - BSS

Where,

$x_1, x_2, x_3,$ are score in different group

C = correction Term

TSS = Total Sum of Squares

BSS = Between Sum of Squares

WSS = Within Sum of Squares

v. CO-EFFICIENT OF CORRELATION (r)

$$r = \frac{n\left(\sum xy\right) - \left(\sum x\right)\sum y}{\sqrt{\left[n\sum x^2 - \left(\sum x\right)^2\right]\left[n\sum y^2 - \left(\sum y\right)^2\right]}}$$

x, y – Variables,

N- Total strength.

CONCLUSION

The chapter outlines the design of the present study, the procedure followed and the nature of the sample. It describes the objective of the study, hypotheses to be tested, the tools to be used and the methods of administration and scoring. The need, significance and delimitations of this present study have also been discussed. The analysis and interpretation of the data will be dealt with elaborately in the next chapter.

❐

14

Analysis and Interpretation of Data

Analysis of data is an important step in quantitative research. According to Mouly (1964), *"Research data become meaningful in the process of being analyzed and interpreted"*. The key phase of every thesis is the proper analysis and interpretation of the data.

This chapter presents the results obtained from the analysis of data collected from the high school who are working in different types (Government, Aided, Private) of schools based on two variables viz., Family Environment and Self Confidence. The data has been subjected to descriptive, differential and correlation analysis.

IMPORTANCE OF DATA ANALYSIS

Analysis of data is an important step in quantitative research

According to Mouly (1964) "Research data becomes meaningful in the process of being analyzed and interpreted". The key phase of every thesis is the proper analysis and interpretation of the data.

According to Gay(1976), " Analysis of the data is important as any other component of the research process"

According to Carter V Good, states "The purpose of interpretation is essentially one of stating what the finding convey? What is their significance? What is the answer to the original problem?

If research is to be productive, the plan for analysis must be laid at the time the study is selected and designed. Unless the analysis of the data can be made sufficiently precise to permit interpretation and generalization there is no point in conducting the investigation. The analysis of research data follows rather closely the development of science, some of the principles of which will be repeated in brief for the sake of community in discussion. A prerequisite to interpretation is experience, which bears on the fundamental problem of obtaining accurate and adequate data, for no conclusion, regardless of the adequacy of analysis can be more accurate than the data on which it is based.

Although quantification is a fundamental step in the analysis and interpretation of data, it is not an end in itself and conclusions must always be interpreted on the basis of the variables being investigated rather than on the basis of the variables of their numerical values. A statistic is an abstraction used to represent a large mass of data – it has no meaning of its own. Thus the analysis of data is essential to make the study more meaningful and reliable.

DESCRIPTIVE ANALYSIS

Hypothesis 1

The level of Family Environment of IX Standard Students is moderate in nature

TABLE. 14.1: Showing the level of Family Environment of IX standard Students

Variable	Level	Range	Frequency	Percentage
Family Environment	Low	Below 228	80	26.7
	Moderate	229 to 259	144	48.0
	High	Above 260	76	25.3

INFERENCE

From the above table it is known that, more number of students are present in the level between 229 to 259, shows that the level of Family Environment of IX standard Students is moderate in nature.Hence the hypothesis 1 is accepted.

Hypothesis 2

The level of Self Confidence of IX standard Students is moderate in nature

TABLE. 14.2: Showing the Level of Self Confidence of IX Standard Students

Variable	Level	Range	Frequency	Percentage
Self - Confidence	Low	Below 23	83	27.7
	Moderate	24 to 29	135	45.0
	High	Above 30	82	27.3

INFERENCE

From the above table it is known that, more number of students are present in the level between 24 to 29, shows that the level of Self Confidence of IX standard Students is moderate in nature. Hence the hypothesis 2 is accepted.

DIFFERENTIAL ANALYSIS

Hypothesis 3

There is no significant difference in Family Environment of IX standard Students based on Gender

TABLE. 14.3: Showing the Mean, Standard Deviation and Critical Ratio value for Family Environment of IX standard Students based on Gender

Variable	Gender	N	Mean	Standard Deviation	C.R value	L.S
Family Environment	Male	150	248.82	29.771	2.599	0.01
	Female	150	240.55	25.129		

INFERENCE

From the above table it is observed that the calculated C.R Value (2.599) is greater than the table value (2.58) at 0.01 level.

Shows that there is significant difference in Family Environment of IX standard Students based on Gender. Hence the hypothesis 3 is rejected.

It is also noted that the Family Environment of the male is greater than female IX standard students.

Hypothesis 4

There is no significant difference in Family Environment of IX standard Students based on Type of School.

TABLE. 14.4: Showing ANOVA for Family Environment among IX standard Students Based on Type of School

Variables	Source of Variance	Sum of Squares	df	Mean Square	'F' Ratio	L.S
Family Environment	Between Groups	4637.830	2	2318.915	3.039	0.01
	Within Groups	226628.72	297	763.060		
	Total	**231266.55**	**299**			

INFERENCE

From the above table it is seen that the calculated 'F' value (3.039) is greater than 'F' Table value (4.68) at 0.01 level.

So it is inferred that there is significant difference in Family Environment among IX standard Students based on Type of School. Hence the hypothesis 4 is rejected.

Further analysis is done and presented in the following table 4.4 (a)

TABLE. 14.4 (A) Showing the Mean, Standard Deviation and Critical Ratio value for Family Environment of IX standard Students based on Type of School

Variable	Type of School	F	Mean	Standard Deviation	C.R Value	L.S
Family Environment	Boys Vs Girls	28	237.68	23.465	0.026	NS
		45	237.80	16.737		
	Girls Vs Co-Education	45	237.80	16.737	1.995	0.01
		227	246.92	29.706		
	Co-Education Vs Boys	227	246.92	29.706	1.585	NS
		28	237.68	23.465		

INFERENCE

From the above table following inferences have been made.

In the first case, the calculated C.R value (0.026) is lower than table value (1.96) at 0.05 level of significance, show that there is no significant difference between Boys and Girls of IX standard with regard to Family Environment.

In the second case, the calculated C.R value (1.995) is higher than the table value (1.96) at 0.01 level of significance, show that there is significant difference between Girls and Co-Education of IX standard with regard to Family Environment.

In the third case, the calculated C.R value (1.585) is lower than the expected table value (1.96) at 0.05 level of significance, shows that there is no significant difference between Co-Education and Boys of IX standard Students with regard to Family Environment.

It is also noted that the Family Environment of the Co-Education is greater than Girls IX standard students

Hypothesis 5

There is no significant difference in Family Environment of High School IX standard Students based on Type of Management

TABLE,14.5: Showing the Mean, Standard Deviation and Critical Ratio value for Family Environment of IX standard Students based on Type of Management

Variable		Sum of Squares	df	Mean Squares	'F' Value	L.S
Family Environment	Between Groups	4799.717	2	2399.858	3.147	0.05
	Within Groups	226466.83	297	762.515		
	Total	**231266.55**	**299**			

INFERENCE

From the above table it is observed that the calculated C.R Value (3.147) is greater than the table value (3.03) at 0.05 level.

Shows that there is significant difference in Family Environment of IX standard Students based on Type of Management. Hence the hypothesis 5 is rejected.

Further analysis is done and presented in the following table 4.5 (a)

TABLE.14.5 (A) Showing the Mean, Standard Deviation and Critical Ratio value for Family Environment of IX standard Students based on Type of Management

Variable	Type of Management	F	Mean	Standard Deviation	C.R Value	L.S
Family Environment	Govt Vs Private	53	240.17	29.596	0.185	NS
		65	239.37	16.617		
	Private Vs Govt Aided	65	239.37	16.617	2.173	0.05
		182	247.90	30.032		
	Govt Aided Vs Govt	182	247.90	30.032	0.971	NS
		53	240.17	29.596		

INFERENCE

From the above table following inference have been made.

In the first case, the calculated C.R value (0.185) is lower than table value (1.96) at 0.05 level of significance, shows that there is no significant difference between students studying in Govt and Private of IX standard with regard to Family Environment .

In the second case, the calculated C.R value (2.173) is higher than the table value (1.96) at 0.05 level of significance, show that there is significant difference between students studying in Private and Govt Aided of IX standard with regard to Family Environment .

In the third case, the calculated C.R value (0.914) is lesser than the table value (1.96) at 0.05 level of significance, shows that there is no significant difference between students studying in Govt Aided and Govt IX standard students with regard to Family Environment.

Hypothesis 6

There is no significant difference in Family Environment of IX standard Students based on Father's Qualification.

TABLE. 14.6: Showing ANOVA for Family Environment of IX Standard Students based on Father's Qualification

Variables	Source of Variance	Sum of Squares	df	Mean Square	'F' Ratio	L.S
Family Environment	Between Groups	1501.992	2	750.996	0.380	N.S
	Within Groups	229764.55	297	773.618		
	Total	**231266.55**	**299**			

INFERENCE

From the above table it is seen that the calculated 'F' Value (0.380) is lesser than table value (3.03) at 0.05 level of significance, so it is inferred that there is no significant difference in Family Environment of IX standard Students based on Father's Qualification.

Hence the hypothesis 6 is accepted.

Hypothesis 7

There is no significant difference in Family Environment of IX standard Students based on Father's Occupation

TABLE. 14.7: Showing ANOVA for Family Environment of IX standard Students Based on Father's Qualification

Variables	Source of Variance	Sum of Squares	df	Mean Square	'F' Ratio	L.S
Family Environment	Between Groups	1660.470	2	830.235	1.074	N.S
	Within Groups	229606.08	297	773.084		
	Total	**231266.55**	**299**			

INFERENCE

From the above table it is seen that the calculated 'F' Value (1.074) is lesser than table value (3.03) at 0.05, so it is inferred that there is no significant difference in Family Environment of IX standard Students based on Father's Qualification. Hence the hypothesis 7 is accepted.

Hypothesis 8

There is no significant difference in Family Environment of IX standard Students based on Mother's Qualification.

TABLE. 14.8: Showing ANOVA for Family Environment of IX standard Students Based on Mother's Qualification

Variables	Source of Variance	Sum of Squares	Df	Mean Square	'F' Ratio	L.S
Family Environment	Between Groups	463.752	2	231.876	0.298	N.S
	Within Groups	230802.79	297	777.114		
	Total	**231266.55**	**299**			

INFERENCE

From the above table it is seen that the calculated 'F' Value (0.298) is lesser than table value (3.03) at 0.05 level of significance, so it is inferred that there is no significant difference in Family Environment of IX standard Students based on Mother's Qualification. Hence the hypothesis 8 is accepted.

Hypothesis 9

There is no significant difference in Family Environment of IX standard Students based on Mother's Occupation.

TABLE. 14.9: Showing ANOVA for Family Environment of IX standard Students based on Mother's Occupation

Variables	Source of Variance	Sum of Squares	Df	Mean Square	'F' Ratio	L.S
Family Environment	Between Groups	1688.976	2	844.488	1.092	NS
	Within Groups	229577.57	297	772.988		
	Total	**231266.55**	**299**			

INFERENCE

From the above table it is seen that the calculated 'F' Value (1.092) is lesser than table value (3.03) at 0.05 level of significance. So it is inferred that there is no significant difference in Family Environment of IX standard Students based on Mother's Occupation. Hence the hypothesis 9 is accepted.

Hypothesis 10

There is no significant difference in Family Environment of IX standard Students based on Type of Family.

TABLE. 14.10: Showing the Mean, Standard Deviation and Critical Ratio value for Family Environment of IX standard Students based on Type of Family

Variable	Gender	F	Mean	Standard Deviation	C.R value	L.S
Family Environment	Joint	81	243.28	25.479	0.531	NS
	Nuclear	219	245.21	28.664		

INFERENCE

From the above table it is observed that the calculated C.R Value (0.531) is lesser than the table value (1.96) at 0.05 level of significance.

Shows that there is no significant difference in Family Environment of IX standard Students based on Type of Family. Hence the hypothesis 10 is accepted.

Hypothesis 11

There is no significant difference in Self Confidence of IX standard Students based on Gender.

TABLE. 14.11: Showing the Mean, Standard Deviation and Critical Ratio value for Self Confidence of IX standard Students based on Gender.

Variable	Gender	F	Mean	Standard Deviation	C.R value	L.S
Self - Confidence	Male	150	27.43	5.916	2.875	0.01
	Female	150	25.64	4.833		

INFERENCE

From the above table it is observed that the calculated C.R Value (2.875) is greater than the table value (2.58) at 0.01 level of significance.

Shows that there is significant difference in Self Confidence of IX standard Students based on Gender. Hence the hypothesis 11 is rejected.

It is also noted that the self confidence of the male is greater than female IX standard students.

Hypothesis 12

There is no significant difference in Self - Confidence of IX standard Students based on Type of School.

TABLE. 14.12: Showing ANOVA for Self Confidence of IX standard Students based on Type of School

Variables	Source of Variance	Sum of Squares	df	Mean Square	'F' Ratio	L.S
Self - Confidence	Between Groups	545.880	2	272.940	9.661	0.01
	Within Groups	8390.717	297	28.252		
	Total	**8936.597**	**299**			

INFERENCE

From the above table it is seen that the calculated 'F' value (9.661) is greater than 'F' Table value (4.68) at 0.01 level of significance.

So it is inferred that there is significant difference in Self - Confidence of High School IX standard Students based on Type of School. Hence the hypothesis 12 is rejected.

Further analysis is done and presented in the following table 4.12 (a)

TABLE. 14.12: (a) Showing the Mean, Standard Deviation and Critical Ratio value for Self Confidence of IX standard Students based on Type of School.

Variable	Type of School	F	Mean	Standard Deviation	C.R Value	L.S
Self Confidence	Boys Vs Girls	28	25.86	3.679	2.509	0.05
		45	23.47	4.121		
	Girls Vs Co-Education	45	23.47	4.121	4.229	0.01
		227	27.23	5.675		
	Co-Education Vs Boys	227	27.23	5.675	1.246	NS
		28	25.86	3.679		

INFERENCE

From the above table following inference have been made.

In the first case, the calculated C.R value (2.509) is greater than table value (1.96) at 0.05 level of significance; show that there is significant difference between Boys and Girls of IX standard students with regard to Self- Confidence.

In the second case, the calculated C.R value (4.229) is greater than the table value (2.58) at 0.01 level of significance, shows that there is significant difference between in Girls and Co-Education of IX standard students with regard to Self Confidence.

In the third case, the calculated C.R value (1.246) is lower than the table value (1.96) at 0.05 level of significance, shows that there is no significant difference between in Co-Education and Boys of IX standard Students with regard to Self Confidence.

It is also noted that the self confidence of the Co-Education is greater than Girls IX standard students.

Hypothesis 13

There is no significant difference in Self Confidence of IX standard Students based on Type of Management.

TABLE. 14.13: Showing the Mean, Standard Deviation and Critical Ratio value for Family Environment of IX standard Students based on Type of Management

Variable		Sum of Squares	df	Mean Squares	'F' Value	L.S
Self - Confidence	Between Groups	479.365	2	239.682	8.417	0.01
	Within Groups	8457.232	297	28.476		
	Total	**8936.597**	**299**			

INFERENCE

From the above table it is observed that the calculated F Value (8.417) is greater than the table value (4.68) at 0.01 level of significance.

Shows that there is significant difference in Family Environment of IX standard Students based on Type of Management. Hence the hypothesis 13 is rejected.

Further analysis is done and presented in the following table 4.13 (a)

TABLE. 14.13 (A) Showing the Mean, Standard Deviation and Critical Ratio value for Self Confidence of IX Students based on Type of Management

Variable	Type of Management	F	Mean	Standard Deviation	C.R Value	L.S
Self - Confidence	Govt Vs Private	53	26.85	4.967	3.195	0.01
		65	24.15	4.195		
	Private Vs Govt Aided	65	24.15	4.195	4.019	0.01
		182	27.30	5.781		
	Govt Aided Vs Govt	182	27.30	5.781	0.511	NS
		53	26.85	4.967		

INFERENCE

From the above table following inference have been made.

In the first case, the calculated C.R value (3.195) is greater than table value (2.58) at 0.01 level of significance, show that there is significant difference between students studying in Govt and Private of high school IX standard with regard to Self - Confidence .

In the second case, the calculated C.R value (4.019) is higher than the table value (2.58) at 0.01 level of significance, showing that there is significant difference between students studying in Private and Government Aided high school IX standard with regard to Self - Confidence .

In the third case, the calculated value (0.511) is lesser than the table value (1.96) at 0.05 level of significance, shows that there is no significant difference between students studying in Government Aided and Government high school IX standard students with regard to Self - Confidence.

Hypothesis 14

There is no significant difference in Self Confidence of IX standard Students based on Father's Qualification.

TABLE. 14.14: Showing ANOVA for Self Confidence of IX standard Students based on Father's Qualification

Variables	Source of Variance	Sum of Squares	df	Mean Square	'F' Ratio	L.S
Self Confidence	Between Groups	127.591	2	63.795	2.151	NS
	Within Groups	8809.006	297	29.660		
	Total	8936.567	299			

INFERENCE

From the above table it is seen that the calculated 'F' Value (2.151) is lesser than table value (3.03) at 0.05 level, so it is inferred that there is no significant difference in Self Confidence of IX standard Students based on Father's Qualification. Hence the hypothesis 14 is accepted.

Hypothesis 15

There is no significant difference in Self Confidence of IX standard Students based on Father's Occupation.

TABLE. 14.15: Showing ANOVA for Self Confidence of IX standard Students based on Father's Occupation

Variables	Source of Variance	Sum of Squares	df	Mean Square	'F' Ratio	L.S
Self Confidence	Between Groups	88.332	2	44.166	1.482	NS
	Within Groups	8848.265	297	29.792		
	Total	**8936.597**	**299**			

INFERENCE

From the above table it is seen that the calculated 'F' Value (1.482) is lesser than table value (3.03) at 0.05 (Level of Significance), so it is inferred that there is no significant difference in Self Confidence of IX standard Students based on Father's Qualification. Hence the hypothesis 15 is accepted.

Hypothesis 16

There is no significant difference in Self Confidence of IX standard Students based on Mother's Qualification.

TABLE. 14.16: Showing ANOVA for Self Confidence of IX standard Students based on Mother's Qualification

Variables	Source of Variance	Sum of Squares	df	Mean Square	'F' Ratio	L.S
Self Confidence	Between Groups	19.168	2	9.584	0.319	NS
	Within Groups	8917.429	297	30.025		
	Total	**8936.597**	**299**			

INFERENCE

From the above table it is seen that the calculated 'F' Value (0.319) is lesser than table value (3.03) at 0.05 (Level of Significance), so it is inferred that there is no significant difference in Self Confidence of IX standard Students based on Mother's Qualification. Hence the hypothesis 16 is accepted.

Hypothesis 17

There is no significant difference in Self Confidence of IX standard Students based on Mother's Occupation.

TABLE. 14.17: Showing ANOVA for Self Confidence of IX standard Students based on Mother's Occupation

Variables	Source of Variance	Sum of Squares	Df	Mean Square	'F' Ratio	L.S
Self Confidence	Between Groups	3.631	2	1.815	0.060	NS
	Within Groups	8932.966	297	30.077		
	Total	**8936.597**	**299**			

INFERENCE

From the above table it is seen that the calculated 'F' Value (0.060) is lesser than table value (3.03) at 0.05 level of significance. So it is inferred that there is no significant difference in Self Confidence of IX standard Students based on Mother's Occupation.

Hence the hypothesis 17 is accepted.

Hypothesis 18

There is no significant difference in Self Confidence of IX standard Students based on Type of Family.

TABLE. 14.18: Showing the Mean, Standard Deviation and Critical Ratio value for Self Confidence of IX standard Students based on Type of Family.

Variable	Gender	F	Mean	Standard Deviation	C.R value	L.S
Self Confidence	Joint	81	26.41	5.108	0.249	NS
	Nuclear	219	26.58	5.604		

INFERENCE

From the above table it is observed that the calculated C.R Value (0.249) is lesser than the table value (1.96) at 0.05 level of significance.

So there is no significant difference in Self - Confidence of IX standard Students based on Type of Family. Hence the hypothesis 18 is accepted.

CORRELATIONAL ANALYSIS

Hypothesis 19

There is no significant correlation between Family Environment and Self Confidence of IX standard Students

TABLE. 14.19: Showing the correlation between Family Environment and Self Confidence of IX standard Students

Variables	Sample	'r' Value	L.S
Family Environment	300	0.396	0.05
Self Confidence			

INFERENCE

Fro the above table, it is clearly observed that the 'r' value is (0.396) is greater than the table value (0.148) of 0.05 level. So there is significant correlation between Family Environment and Self Confidence. Hence the hypothesis 19 is rejected. It also indicates that there is positive correlation between Family Environment and Self Confidence

CONCLUSION

The analysis and interpretation of data represent the application of deductive and inductive logic to the research process. The data are often classified by division into subgroups and the analyzed and synthesized in such a way that hypothesis may be accepted and rejected. The final result may be a new principle or generalization. Like interpretation of results, the formulation of conclusion and generalization also demands keen observations, wide outlook and power logical thinking. A brief report of the present research study together with major finding and conclusion has been presented in the succeeding chapter. ❐

15

Summary, Findings and Conclusion

This chapter deals with the consolidation of the various findings presented in the previous chapter findings are statements of factual information based upon data analysis. Conclusion is answers to the questions raised or the statements of acceptance or rejection of the hypotheses proposed. In this chapter the researcher deals with the aspects pertaining to the tools used for the investigations, objectives and hypotheses of the study, based on analysis the major findings arrived at, and all finally the educational implication together with suggestion for further research. The aim of the present investigation is to study Family Environment and Self Confidence among IX standard school students.

STATEMENT OF THE PROBLEM

The present study has been entitled as *"Family Environment and Self Confidence among IX standard students"*.

OBJECTIVES OF THE STUDY

The following objectives are set in the present study.

1. To find out the level of Family Environment of IX standard students.
2. To find out the level of Self- Confidence of IX standard students.

3. To find out the significant difference in the Family Environment of IX standard students based on Gender.
4. To find out the significant difference in the Family Environment of IX standard students based on Type of School
5. To find out the significant difference in the Family Environment of IX standard students based on Type of Management.
6. To find out the significant difference in the Family Environment of IX standard students based on Father's Qualification
7. To find out the significant difference in the Family Environment of IX standard students based on Father's Occupation.
8. To find out the significant difference in the Family Environment of IX standard students based on Mother's Qualification.
9. To find out the significant difference in the Family Environment of IX standard students based on Mother's Occupation.
10. To find out the significant difference in the Family Environment of IX standard students based on Type of Family.
11. To find out the significant difference in the Self Confidence of IX standard students based on Gender
12. To find out the significant difference in the Self Confidence of IX standard students based on Type of School
13. To find out the significant difference in the Self Confidence of IX standard students based on Type of Management.
14. To find out the significant difference in the Self Confidence of IX standard students based on Father's Qualification
15. To find out the significant difference in the Self Confidence of IX standard students based on Father's Occupation.
16. To find out the significant difference in the Self Confidence of IX standard students based on Mother's Qualification.
17. To find out the significant difference in the Self Confidence of IX standard students based on Mother's Occupation.
18. To find out the significant difference in the Self Confidence of IX standard students based on Type of Family.

HYPOTHESES OF THE STUDY

1. The hypotheses formed in the present study are listed below:
2. To find out the level of Self- Confidence of IX standard students.
3. To find out the significant difference in the Family Environment of IX standard students based on Gender.
4. To find out the significant difference in the Family Environment of IX standard students based on Type of School

5. To find out the significant difference in the Family Environment of IX standard students based on Type of Management.
7. To find out the significant difference in the Family Environment of IX standard students based on Father's Qualification
8. To find out the significant difference in the Family Environment of IX standard students based on Father's Occupation.
9. To find out the significant difference in the Family Environment of IX standard students based on Mother's Qualification.
10. To find out the significant difference in the Family Environment of IX standard students based on Mother's Occupation.
11. To find out the significant difference in the Family Environment of IX standard students based on Type of Family.
12. To find out the significant difference in the Self Confidence of IX standard students based on Gender
13. To find out the significant difference in the Self Confidence of IX standard students based on Type of School
14. To find out the significant difference in the Self Confidence of IX standard students based on Type of Management.
15. To find out the significant difference in the Self Confidence of IX standard students based on Father's Qualification
16. To find out the significant difference in the Self Confidence of IX standard students based on Father's Occupation.
17. To find out the significant difference in the Self Confidence of IX standard students based on Mother's Qualification.
18. To find out the significant difference in the Self Confidence of IX standard students based on Mother's Occupation.
19. To find out the significant difference in the Self Confidence of IX standard students based on Type of Family.
20. To find out the significant difference in there is positive correlation between Family Environment and Self Confidence.

TOOLS USED BY THE INVESTIGATOR

The general category of inquiry forms includes data includes data-gathering instruments through which responds answer questions or respond to statements in writing, 'questionnaire' is used to collect factual information from the target population. In the present study,

To test the hypotheses formulated, the following tools have been used in the present study.

1. Personal data sheet developed by the investigator (Appendix I)

2. Family Environment Scale by Harrpreet Bhatia and Chadha N.K (1993) was adopted (Appendix II)
3. Self Confidence Assessment Scale (SCAS) constructed and validated by Suresh Kumar. M and Vaiyauri Raja. M (2010) adopted (Appendix III)

MAJOR FINDINGS

Based on the analysis of the data, the major findings are listed below.

1. It was found that the level of Family Environment IX Standard Students is moderate in nature.
2. It was found that the level of Self Confidence IX Standard Students is moderate in nature.
3. It was found that the Male and female students of IX Standard Students do not differ significantly in Family Environment regards to Gender.
4. It was found that the Boys, Girls and Co-Education of IX Standard Students differ significantly in Family Environment regards to Type of School.
5. It was found that the Government, Government Aided and Private of IX Standard Students differ significantly in Family Environment regards to Type of Management.
6. It was found that the Illiterate, School and College of IX Standard Students do not differ significantly in Family Environment regards to Father's Qualification.
7. It was found that the Government, Private and Daily Wages of IX Standard Students do not differ significantly in Family Environment regards to Father's Occupation.
8. It was found that the Illiterate, School and College of IX Standard Students do not differ significantly in Family Environment regards to Mother's Qualification.
9. It was found that the Government, Private and Daily Wages of IX Standard Students do not differ significantly in Family Environment regards to Mother's Occupation.
10. It was found that the Nuclear and Joint Family of IX Standard Students do not differ significantly in Family Environment regards to Type of Family.
11. It was found that the Male and female students of IX Standard Students differ significantly in Self-Confidence regards to Gender.
12. It was found that the Boys, Girls and Co-Education of IX Standard Students do not differ significantly in Self-Confidence regards to Type of School.

13. It was found that the Government, Government Aided and Private of IX Standard Students differ significantly in Self-Confidence regards to Type of Management.
14. It was found that the Illiterate, School and College of IX Standard Students do not differ significantly in Self-Confidence regards to Father's Qualification.
15. It was found that the Government, Private and Daily Wages of IX Standard Students do not differ significantly in Self-Confidence regards to Father's Occupation.
16. It was found that the Illiterate, School and College of IX Standard Students do not differ significantly in Self-Confidence regards to Mother's Qualification
17. It was found that the Government, Private and Daily Wages of IX Standard Students do not differ significantly in Self-Confidence regards to Mother's Occupation
18. It was found that the Nuclear and Joint Family of IX Standard Students do not differ significantly in Self-Confidence regards to Type of Family
19. It was found that the there is no significant positive correlation between Family Environment and Self-Confidence of higher secondary school students.

EDUCATIONAL IMPLICATIONS & RECOMMENDATIONS

The findings of the present investigation are important for the improvement in the Quality of education, Family Environment being an important aspect of human behaviour throws light on the behaviour of the higher secondary students. Family Environment is also an ability which plays a major role in life. The following are some of the major recommendations to improve the Family Environment and Self - Confidence of the students. Parents could be the proper motivator to develop Family Environment among the higher secondary school students through the process of guiding, directing, stimulating arid encouraging at every step. Most of the programmes in school are heavily oriented towards information sharing rather than encouraging and developing Family Environment. Therefore it is a felt need to review and modify the programmes in school.

Family Environment helps the students to improve their self or worth value and develop the right attitude towards society and this in future would help them become better persons. This positive attitude automatically increases their achievement level. This increase in Family Environment also helps the students to mould themselves into a better personality.

This further help those to be flexible with their friends and fellow beings which pave the way for unity in diversity .Since teachers play a vital role in the development process of any individual, early identification and environment stimulation related to Family Environment can be provided. The teachers should adopt modern teaching strategies and methods in the class room to give opportunities required for the enhancement of these qualities could be developed

By organizing workshops, conference, seminars and also including the aspect within the curriculum among the schools. Development of Family Environment among school students is a different complex task. In schools there should be lot of scope for participation in different programme, curricular and co-curricular activities. Children should be encouraged to participate in all programmes, since they offer scope for developing Flexible manner, Tolerance and Self evaluation ability among the individuals. Self - Confidence among the students may also be attributed to over work load on the students. Sometimes the incapability to cope up with such pressure may also cause for the lowering of the Family Environment among them. The teacher can train the students with various coping strategies, which can help the students overcome their Self - Confidence.

The students can be given physical activities like performing physical exercise, involving them in few games etc. which can serve stress busters. Teachers can provide necessary counselling to the first generation learners and low achievers which can levels and also their Self - Confidence, thereby leading to better academic achievement and aspiration.

DELIMITATIONS OF THE STUDY

The present study had the following delimitations

- Only high school students were chosen for investigation.
- The sample has been chosen from Trichy District.
- The sample is confined into 300, due to lack of time.

SUGGESTIONS FOR THE FURTHER RESEARCH

Following are some of the suggestion put forward by the investigator for further research

1. This study was concentrated only on high school students. Similar study could be extended to Higher Secondary school students.
2. The study was conducted only in a few selected schools in Trichy. It can be extended to many other schools and in many districts.
3. A comprehensive study of this type involving different standards of students at various levels could also be under taken.

4. A similar study of the present investigation could be done with other related variables.
5. The study is confined to only 300 IX standard students of Trichy District. Further studies can be conducted on other districts.

CONCLUSION

The purpose of the study was to study the relationship among the variables viz., Family Environment and Self Confidence. The study is sure to find some usefulness in the field of education and findings of the investigator can serve as a database for further research.

❐

16

Invariable Fears of Teachers

Stress has been acknowledged inherent in the process of teaching. Most teachers, howsoever bright, well read, experienced and well prepared experience some amount of stress while going to lecture in front of the student, but manage to handle it. It is also true that some feel more stressed than others and face occasional difficulty in coping with it. Some teachers find it quite heavy on them and extremely difficult carry on the work, as they are not able to either structure the work environment or exercise control over the factors underlying the stress, or to enhance their capability to cope. It then threatens to adversely impact their physical health reduces their teaching commitment and effectiveness to the extent of their needing professional help. Prolonged periods of intense stress, if not taken care of, can produce feelings of emotional exhaustion, reduce personal accomplishment, induce a sense of professional failure, and even a tendency to act with the clientele in a depersonalized manner, the symptoms which define burnout. Stress and burnout among teachers found directly influence their functioning and survival in the system, and quality of educational and related services offered to all students, and without exception for those with special needs.

STRESS AND BURNOUT IN INDIAN CONTEXT

As stated in the introduction and other subsequent places in the book, although the definitional complexities in the assessment of stress and burnout are enormous and difficult to be resolved in general. An additional problem has been confronted by researchers in the understanding and assessment of stress and burnout in educational institutions of south Asia because of the specific cultural values of obedience of authority, nurturance of the young, etc. The socio-cultural situations have though, undergone gradual changes in the post independence period, and the difficulty of such unmet unconditional expectations now characterize the numerous interpersonal problems at all levels from administrative heads to students. The emotional strains of interpersonal emotional distances and the non-reciprocal relationships among different sections often operate at the latent level, and camouflage the severity of stress effects.

Like many of the educational institutions in south Asia, teachers in contemporary Indian schools are confronted with the reality of diverse social groups of educators and pupils, large size of class and raised expectations , leaving for them little scope and time for personal interaction with students and colleagues. Over the years, as social power and money have become important personal and social values, and the new professions have emerged, the teaching profession has got devalued. Teachers do not have the desired social respect, nor do they get adequate financial rewards/support for their work. Teachers expected to confer knowledge, and make every child the best achiever in every domain of activity. The task is challenging and demanding, but the teachers represent a mixed lot, with varied levels of skills, capabilities, resources, etc. Teachers who are capability and good, generally respected and appreciated, but instances are uncommon, when parents and students alike so not give a hot to the teachers, and blame them for any shortcomings observed in children/ school. Many parents do not wish their child to be a teacher. Many (parents, husbands and in-laws) view teaching as an ideal profession for women, as they can finish their work by the afternoon and take care of their home and children (a part time employee on full salary).

There has been little research in the Indian schools in areas of teacher concerns, stress and burnout. The first and School Surveys of Research in Education (Buch, 1974, 1979) did not include any study on teacher stress and burnout. A later bibliography (Dave and Murry, 1933) included three studies, each emphasizing a different aspect of burnout. As the pressures to perform from various quarters continue to rise, despite the adverse conditions of functioning of teaching institutions, teachers need familial and social support in differentiating across variety of stresses and in handling the day to day stresses, and thus prevent burnout.

INTRODUCTION: SETTING THE SCENE

Stress, burnout and coping researches have been confining for years to clinical areas, and the terms have acquired negative connotations, with which the inflicted struggled in a bid to find relief, and in the process depleted and/or exhausted the resources under their control. This indicates an unquestionable acceptance of the underlying assumption of persons going through the stressful experiences, having no control/volition or an alternative path out, and thus the need of therapy. The common experience as well as the evidence from research does not validate it. There neither is adequate logical ground to argue and suggest that all types of stress are necessarily negative and unhealthy for ones functioning, nor are the stress and burnout equivalents. A distinction been made in the literature between positive and negative stress, and between stress and burnout. Positive stress called eustress, and negative stress labelled distress. In fact, the positive affect has not been entirely neglected in the classical models of stress either. It has been discussed in relation to the (a) primary appraisal of stressful situations as challenges, which signal the probability of makings gains and characterized by positive emotions, like eagerness, excitement, and confidence. (b) Appraisal of the resolution of a stressful encounter as successful leading to emotions of happiness and pride. (c) Cessation of aversive conditions, when people are likely to experience an offsetting positive emotion, such as relief, and (d) Examining of the other positive outcomes of stressful events, even if the events have not been favorably resolved. The positive outcomes may include perceived benefits of stressful encounters, newly acquired skills and resources that may help in coping, and spiritual/religious transformation in thinking and attitudes.

MEANING OF STRESS

Stress is a condition stream on ones emotions, thought processes and physical conditions. When it is excessive, it can pretend once ability to cope with environment. (Hans Selye, 1976) "Stress is the general term applied to the pressures; employs developed various symptoms of stress as, "an adjective demand placed on the organism".

From the above definitions, it may understand that stress pretends the wellbeing of the organism; conditions that tend to because stress called pressure. In this age of anxiety, stress considered as an inevitable aspect of human life, forcing him to cope up with it for successful and happy life. The main factors of creating stress in individual are Biological, Psychological and Socio-Cultural. Biological factors influence all aspects of our behavior including our intellectual capabilities, basic temperament, primary reaction tendencies and stress tolerance. Psychosocial factors of stress also influence the well-being of the individual in contemporary life. Stress due to failure, losses, personal limitations, guilt and loneliness leads to self-deviation. Modern living is a bundle load of pressures acting on individuals. Each individual experience his own unique pattern of pressures such as competing with others, meeting educational, occupational, and marital depends and coping with the complexity and in rapid pace of modern life . There are other socio-cultural factors creating stress on modern man such as problems of war and violence, group prejudice and discrimination, economic and unemployment problems, rapid social change existential anxiety.

JOB STRESS

In this last decade of twentieth century, many people are unable to cope up with stress generated because of circumstances forcing them to adopt fact-paced life styles. This position is highly significant when people are at work. A rational and logical inference one can make, now basing on the above premises is that working styles are also subjected to change in accordance to the fast changing life styles, mat be a presupposition for work stress or job stress. Therefore, job stress has received an increasing concern to the researchers in the areas of organizational behavior and social psychology, who have been undertaking evidences about the effects of stress on the organization, worker output, and the physical and emotional well-being of the worker.

TEACHERS STRESS

Job stress is the most common psychological phenomena that are prevalent among people who are in different jobs and professions. The stress studies are initially directed toward industrial organization. With the private sector. Researchers have come to believe that stress may be especially prevalent among human service professions, particularly the teaching profession, (Kryacou and Suteliffe 1977-78; Pettigrew and Wolf 1982, Cherniss 1980; and Cooper and Marshall 1980). As teaching is a human service profession, stress within the teaching profession is considerable and may have far-reaching consequences on the entire education system. Teaching is a complex process were in teacher is expected to exhibit many skills. This makes a teacher to experience stress in the profession.

Further Pettergrew and Wolf (1982) opined, “Teacher stress has a Nation-wide concern and relatively new area of empirical research”. Concerns regarding stress among schoolteacher have been raised for over 40 years (Tunk, Meeks and Turk 1982) stress is considered very significant in any educative process much attention is not drawn towards this. Teacher behavior and his performance, classroom interactions, school and classroom climate may consider as the important components of any educative process. It is not easy to ascertain sources of teacher stress, as its ambit is unlimited. However, several attempts are made to identify the sources that possible, create stress among teachers. Factors prepared by teachers as being troublesome or stressful have included students displine, negative student attitudes towards school, physical violence, is adequate preparation time, lack of clear role definition and heavy workloads". (Bearly, Myette and serna, 1983;Chichen and Koff, 1978;Gollady and Noel 1978;Olanderand Ferrel, 1970).

Further Kaiser and Polezynsky (1982) identified factors within educators themselves as a potential source of excess stress. Quick and Quick (1979) proposed four groups of factors creating work stress. They are 1) Role factors, 2) Job factors, 3) Physical factors and 4) Interpersonal factors. A heap of literature available on job stress identified main sources such as job setting, organizational, situational, lack of control over work, co-workers etc.

Teacher is subjected to stress due to incoherent social life, widening social distance, segregation, lack of social support, corruption, nepotism, unnecessary societal involvement in day-to-day activities, high degree of social indiscipline, deterioration of values, lack of social security etc. Besides the potential stress that occurs outside the school, there are also those associated with the school itself. Teaching as a profession demands continuous growth, but teachers while discharging time for further studies, unable to utilize the training the salaries, lack of opportunity for reading training, less change for further promotion etc. are acting as source of stress on teachers.

Teaching as an occupation, present certain situation where in the teacher has to adjust to unhealthy school atmosphere, lack of recognition, for effective teaching. Teaching the subject is which he is not interested, lack of support for innovative approaches, lack of enthusiasm in staff meeting, monotonous working conditions, difference of opinions with head of the institution etc., are the situations acting as sources of stress.

Student behavior is also a major component in the teaching learning process. Continuous misbehavior or certain students, non-acceptance of teacher's authority indiscipline in the class, lack of interest on outsides. Threat from the students, lack of attention in the class, unable to estimate the student, lack of positive responses from the student etc., are some of the significant sources of stress on teachers. Thus, student as a group can be a significant source of teacher stress. Similarly lack of group cohesiveness in school, lack of social support and interpersonal conflicts create teacher stress.

So far, extra organizational, organizational and group stressors are discussed; teacher is the ultimate consumer of stress due to previously mentioned stressors. Thus individual dispositions such as role conflict and ambiguity at organizational and group levels, causes stress. Teachers have to play multiple roles and these often make conflicting expectation. In the present education system heavy expectation are there on teachers. Hence, teachers are supposed to undertake high magnitude of work. Now teachers are experiencing stress as they are supposed to teach more periods a day without rest between periods, excess correction work, undertaking institutional work like censes lack of time for completing syllabus, conduct of co-curricular and extracurricular activities etc.

EFFECTS OF TEACHER STRESS

As job stress effect organizational performance, teacher stress impedes teacher performance in teaching. Infect it is assumed that mild stress can even enhance performance but high level of stress can create physical, Psychological and behavioral problems among teacher. There are several research studies, which observed that, a high level of stress accompanied by physical illness such as high blood pressures, ulcers and even cancer. Similarly high level of stress may be accompanied by psychological problems such as anger, anxiety, depression, nervousness, irritability, tension and boredom. Excessive stress may also result in behavioral problems such as sleeplessness, under eating or over eating, increased smoking and drinking and drug abuse. Many researches of teacher studies have established some strong correlates of teacher stress. From these researches, it has found that teacher stress related to job dissatisfaction (Rudd and Wiseman 1962; Krysacon and Suteliff 1979). Absenteeism, (Bridger 1980; Kaiser and Polezynsky 1982); greater intention to leave profession (Kryiacon and Suteliff 1979), Physical Distress (Coats and Thoresen, 1979) and teacher performance (Kkryiacon and Sutcliffe 1977-79, Pettegrew and Wolf 1982, Kaiser and Polezynsky 1982, Soloman 1960).

However, teaching competency has been recognized as important component of teaching learning process, relatively little effort is made to define the term. A peep in into the literature of teacher effectiveness as one finds many related terms such as teaching success; successful teacher, teaching efficiency, teacher performance, teacher competency etc. "As one looks through heap of investigations in this field" Writes Barr (1961), "One finds various terms used to designate or describe the successful teacher. Frequently the word 'efficiency' is used one will not that the terms are sometimes applied to teacher as in teacher efficiency and sometimes in the teacher behavior as in the teaching efficiency.

Donald M. Medley (1982) States that the teacher competency as those of knowledge, abilities and beliefs on teacher processes and brings to the teaching situation. Teaching competency differs from teacher performance and teacher effectiveness in that it is a stable characteristic of the teacher that does not change appreciably when the teacher moves from one situation to another. By this, it is evident that the knowledge of subject matter, teaching skills, beliefs and feelings of teacher may be considered as the components of teaching competent that a competent teacher is supposed to process.

Biddle (1964) advocates that "disagreement and ambiguity with respect to the description of teaching competence are to be expected and cannot entirely be avoided because competent teaching as undoubtedly a relative matter. Some investigators to refer to training process, properties of teachers, behavior exhibited by teacher and effects produced by teachers, have used the term competence. The same variable have been termed by other investigators as effectiveness, criteria of competency, ability in reach and a host of other terms-teacher success, teacher effectiveness, teacher efficiency, teacher performance, teacher competency etc., are used synonymously by investigators.

Researchers study teacher effectiveness in three component, presage, process and product. Here the presage component refers to thought processes, training aspect and personality factors of the teachers. The process component effects produced by teachers, the same variable have been termed by other investigators as effectiveness, criteria of competency, ability in reach and a host of other terms-teacher success, teacher effectiveness, teacher efficiency, teacher performance, teacher competency etc., are used synonymously by investigators.

Ryan (1960) States, "What constitutes effective teaching?" What are the distinguishing characteristics of competent teacher? are provocative and running questions unfortunately, no universally acceptable definite answers can be given to these complex queries-embarrassing as it may be for professional educators to recognize relatively little progress has been made."

Similarly, Biddle and Ellena accepted in 1966 that nobody knows what a competent teacher was. They said, "Probably no aspect of education has been discussed with greater frequency with as much deep concern or by more educators and citizens. The teacher effectiveness-How to define it, how to identify it, how to measure it, how to evaluate it, and how to detect and remove obstacles to its achievement-finding about the competence of teachers are inconclusive and peace meal and little is presently known for certain about teacher excellence. Researchers study teacher effectiveness in three components; presage, process and product. Here the presage component refers to thought processes, training aspects and personality factors of the teachers. The process component to the teacher's action or classroom practices and the product component refer to the quality of the products i.e. students predicted.

Jangira (1979) states, "teacher's effectiveness has been considered into its three separate components for convenience of presentation. It should be taken that these components are watertight compartment. It also fallow that there are no clear-cut lines to distinguish one component from the other.

TEACHER COMPETENCY AND STRESS

The study is about teacher competency in relation to stress. Teacher competency, in general sense impedes, when teacher suffers from stress. In this chapter, a discussion is made about teacher competency, stress, and the development of this type of study in the world.

TEACHER COMPETENCY

One of the most difficult problems in educational research is that of recognizing teacher competency of discriminating between more and less effective teachers. The role of the classroom teacher in educational is central. The teacher is, after all, the point at contact between the educational system and the pupil. The impact of any educational programme or innovation on the pupil operates through the pupil's teacher. It is therefore quite accurate to say that a school's competence depends on the competence of its teachers. Maximizing teacher competence is a major goal of education. "Teacher competency" refers to the behavior of a teacher while teaching a class (both inside and outside the classroom).Teacher performance differs from teacher competence. It is defined in terms of teacher behavior, of what the teacher does, teacher performance resembles teacher competence in that it is a product of interaction between certain teacher characteristics and the teaching situation-teacher performance is often used as a basis from which teacher competence can be inferred.

"Teacher competence" refers to the set of knowledge, abilities and beliefs a teacher process and bring to the teaching situation Teacher competence differs from teacher performance and teacher effectiveness in that it is a stable characteristic of the teacher that does not change appreciably when the teacher moves from one situation to another. It resembles teacher performance in that it has also been proposed as a basis from which teacher effectiveness can be inferred.

Early Research: The first recorded study of teacher competence (Kratz, 1896), one of the earliest pieces of educational research of any kind to appear, set a design precedent that was to be followed for many years. A large group of elementary school pupils was asked to try to remember the best teacher each of them had ever encountered to write down what made that teacher different from others. Their descriptions were then collated and compared and from them was derived a list of characteristics that supposedly distinguished effective teachers from in effective ones. For the next half-century of so this kind of study was repeact6e again and again with groups chosen in various ways; sometime the task was performed by pupils currently attending schools sometimes by persons considered to be exports, educators, or teacher educators. Perhaps the most extensive and sophisticated example of this was the monumental common wealth teachers training study. (Charters of Waples 1929), which is used exhaustive and meticulous procedures to produce a number of lists of lengths. Typical of the characteristics listed were the following, which were the top six on a list of twenty-five.

1. Adaptability
2. Considerateness
3. Enthusiasm
4. Good judgment
5. Honesty
6. Magnetism

Pupil learning is a direct outcome of pupil learning experiences; learning is after all, something that pupils do not something teachers do. When a teacher "teacher' what she or he really does is try to provide certain learning experiences for the pupils that all expected to bring about desired learning out-comes.

Whatever the nature of the teachers performance, different pupils will have different learning experiences and will make different amounts of gain. Since the unit of study in the process-product model of the class, not the pupil, learning outcomes must be measured in terms of class mean gain before they can be correlated with teacher performance, and variations in gain made by different pupils with the same class must be related as errors that attitude the correlations obtains.

DISSATISFACTION, STRESS AND BURNOUT

Do schools personnel have high moral and are they satisfied in their work setting? Newspaper headlines that emphasize teacher strikes, teacher burnout and stress on school employees suggest that many teachers are not satisfied. A number of studies conducted throughout the 1970s and into the 111980s indicate a gradual reduction in teacher satisfaction (for example, Fuller and Miskel (1972) found that about 89 percent of the teachers participating in this study were satisfied or very satisfied with their job. However, Bentzen, Williams and Heckman (1980), in an investigation conducted in the late 1970s, reported that slightly more than 75 percent of the teachers were satisfied with their jobs. In the later study, important difference in job satisfaction was discovered at the various levels of teaching, with elementary teachers expressing more satisfaction with their jobs than secondary teachers do. A nationwide poll of teachers conducted by the National Educational Association (NBA) in 1980 ("Teachers opinion poll: job satisfaction "1980) found that 35 percent of all public schoolteachers were dissatisfied with their current jobs. Two-fifths of the teacher said they would probably not become teachers if they had it to do all over again; one teacher in ten was planning to leave teaching as soon as possible, and another two teachers in ten were undecided about how long they would remain in teaching. These studies suggest a moderate trend in the direction of increasing dissatisfaction on the part of teachers-although a majority of school personnel continues to express satisfaction with this work.

SYMPTOMS AND CAUSES OF STRESS

Symptoms of teacher dissatisfaction and low morale vary. They include questioning and criticizing of school goals and polices, lack of enthusiasm for teaching rejection or lack of follow- up on administrative directives (Cook, 1979), absenteeism (Educational Research Service, 1980) and fragmentation, that is, a general feeling of being pulled in different directions (Klugman, Cartes &Israel, 1979). Some of these symptoms are also reported in a study by Staplenton, Craft and Frankiewicz (1979).

These researches found a positive relationship between teacher job satisfaction and teacher brink man ship, which they defined as teacher behavior that attempts to challenge the authority structure of the school while attempting to avoid its negative sanctions.

The causes of teacher stress and burnout are not easy to as certain nor are they easily distinguishable from the symptoms, although there is no shortage of suggested causes. With regard to teacher stress, quick and quick (1979) believe that four group of factors create work stress.1) Role factors 2) job factors 3) physical factors and 4) interpersonal factors. They recommended a number of techniques for reducing the stress related by the various factors. The New York State United Teachers Organization that the most important factors contributing to stress is the effect of disruptive children, incompetent administrators are identifies as the second most important cause of stress ("Urban teachers report more stress", 1980).

In the New York stud, urban teachers reported more stress than did sub urban or rural teachers. Cichon and Koff, (1980) found in their research on Chicago teachers that the more important causes of teacher stress are problems of disruption and threats to the teacher's, physical professional and personal well being. In this connection, in NEA survey of its membership in 1980("teacher opinion poll attacks on teacher",1980)estimated that 1,13,000 of the country's 21,84,000 public school teachers were physically attacked by students during a recent twelve month period. Suggested causes of teaches burnout are usually believed to those associated with stress (block, 1978;weiskopt,1980).In a personal account of teacher burnout, Bardol (1979) has described several symptoms and perceived causes.

A number of investigations into the causes of teacher dissatisfaction have been conducted. An NEA survey ("teacher opinion poll; job satisfaction",

1980), found that a majority of teachers felt that the following factors, listed in order of frequency of identification had agentive of feet on their job satisfaction. 1. Public attitudes toward the school. 2. treatment of education by the media.3. Student attitudes toward learning. 4. Salary and 5. Status of teachers in the community. In addition, 49 per cent of the teachers indicated that student behavior had negative effect upon their job satisfaction.

Ford (1979) believe that variables faculty workloads may be related to teacher dissatisfaction between class size and teacher satisfaction is investigated (Glass, et al., 1979,Pages and price (1980)discovered in their study of 130 teachers that the factors contributing most to job dissatisfaction are in order of important.1.lack of planning time. 2. Tedious paper and clerical work 3.On out of tough and autocratic administration.4. Disruptive and unmotivated student's 5.Non teaching activities, such as faculty meeting and "time wasting" workshop 6.Uncooperative parents 7.Lack of autonomy to prescribe curriculum 8.Feeling of failure and 9.Low occupational prestige.

Thus, a brief discussion and outline is presented in the chapter about matters relating to teacher competency and stress. Thus, this kind of analysis gave the investigator. Some clues on the subject on the hand.

❒

17

Review of the Related Literature

The investigator reviewed the available related literature pertaining to teacher stress and teaching competency for the present study and presented as follows.

1. Studies related to Teacher stress.
2. Studies related to Teaching competency.

STUDIES RELATED TO TEACHER STRESS

A study of meaning in life, Stress and Burnout in Teachers of Secondary Schools in Calcutta.

OBJECTS OF THE STUDY

1. To study if teachers varied in the degree of overall meaning in life and if they showed a trend low or high meaning.
2. To identify important sources of meaning in the personal and professional life of teachers and to investigate if teachers varied in the degree of meaning derived from these sources.
3. To find out the relationship, if any among the different measures of meaning in life.
4. To identify the main sources of stress in teaching and to investigate if teachers varied in the extent of experienced stress.

5. To study if teachers varied in the extent of perceived.
6. To study the relationship between stress and burnout meaning

The tools used for data collection were Moholick's (1969) purpose in life Test, Mastach and Jackson (1981) inventory for study of burnout and a scale and interview schedules prepared by the investigator for measurement of stress and other background variables. The sample comprised 345 teachers from 15 secondary schools and an in service teachers Population of three teacher training institutions in Calcutta. Survey and case study techniques were followed in the conduct of the study. Descriptive and non-parametric statistical techniques were used for analysis of data.

FINDINGS THE STUDY

1. Meaningfulness of life of the teachers was quite high according to their own perception.
2. Meaning in professional life was derived primarily from psychic reward obtained from task related outcomes and relationship with the student.
3. All the measures of meaning in life namely self reported meaning in life, source of meaning in life and sources of meaning in teaching had a political relationship with meaning of life.
4. The relationship between stress studied through test and stress reported by teachers was highly significant.
5. Age difference was significant with regard to stress of teachers.
6. The sample teachers had a lower degree of burnout.
7. Sex difference was significant on the burnout variable.
8. Stress was positively related to burnout with regard to emotional exhaustion and depersonalization.
9. There was negative relationship between meaning in life and stress variables measured by tests as well as self – reporting items.
10. A comparatively low level of meaning in life was identified among the sample teachers.

STUDIES RELATED TO TEACHING COMPETENCY

L.S.VERNE.M.R.,L.V.C.U.1985

A STUDY OF SOME OF THE PERSONALITY COMPONENT OF CREATIVE STUDENT TEACHERS IN RELATION TO THEIR COMPETENCE TOWARDS TEACHING.

The study was designed to compare high, medium and low creative student teachers on three dimensions of creativity and total creativity in terms of certain personality components sex, Teaching competence and achievement levels. The sample consisted of 210 B.Ed., students randomly select from our educational instructions in Lucknow. Data regarding creative were collected with the help of tolerance Test of creative thinking. For assessment personality characteristics, the multivariate personality inventory and 16PF were administered to the student teachers. A teacher effectiveness scale was administered to get an idea about their effectiveness as teachers and division scored by them in practice teaching was taken as the criterion of their performance as teachers.

MAIN FINDINGS OF THE STUDY

1. The F ratio for the effect of fluency was significant for dominance-reserved vs. outgoing, humble vs. assertive and tough-minded vs. tender minded.
2. The F ratio for the main effects of flexibility were significant for ego ideal, dominance, sober vs. happy-go-luck and group-dependent vs. self-sufficient.
3. The F ratio for the effect of originality was significant for self-confidence humble vs. assertive and sober vs. happy-go-lucky.
4. The F ratio for the effect of total creativity were significant for empathy, self confidence, reserved vs. outgoing sober vs. happy-go-lucky and taught minded vs. tender minded.
5. The F ratio for the interaction of sex and total creativity was significant for neuroticism, self confidence and reserved vs. outgoing
6. Personality factors distinguishing the low total creativity group from the medium total creativity group were self-confidence, thought minded vs. tender minded and sober vs. happy-go-luck.

NATARAJAN.S. MADRAS-U

A competency based Program in Teacher Education Curriculum:
The major objectives of these investigations were;

1. To study the relative efficiency of competency based teacher education in the pre-service education program of secondary school teachers.
2. To identify factors influencing competency achievement such as social status, economic status and level of education and.
3. To find out the relationship between an individual's self-esteem and competency achievement.

MAJOR FINDINGS OF THE STUDY

1. Competency-based instruction proved suitable for teaching selected units in institutions, planning and administration.
2. The seminar method seemed to be an effective method as it compared favourable with the competency-based approach.

3. The lecture method was effective as a group method.
4. Directed self-study did not compare well with other methods.
5. There was a significant relation between self-esteem and acquisition of competencies.
6. Attitude towards teaching methods had a favorable correlation with acquisition of competencies.
7. The study proved that teacher education programme could be made more effective through a competency-based approach.

BHALWANKARA.G.

- SNDT COLLEGE OF EDUCATION-PUNE-1984
- SIE MAHARASTRA FINANCED

A Study of Reliability and Validity of the Process-Process Appraising Scale of Teacher of Effectiveness.

THE MAJOR OBJECTIVES OF THE STUDY:

1. To determine the reliability of the process-process appraising scale of teacher.
2. To determine criterion related to and the content validity of the PASTE.
3. To determine the relationship between various component scores of PASTE teacher effectiveness scores on PASTE.
4. To study the effect of increase or decrease in number of components of PASTE on reliability and
5. To determine the relationship between presage variables and teacher effectiveness scores of student teacher.

THE MAJOR FINDINGS OF THE STUDY

1. The reliability of PASTE by four-way analysis of variance was 0.72; the reliability of PASTE was quite satisfactory.
2. PASTE had satisfactory content and criterion related validity.
3. All the components correlated positively with the total teacher 3effectiveness score some skills were significant related to total teacher effectiveness.

MAJOR OBJECTIVES OF THE STUDY

1. To compare teacher effectiveness of Male and Female teachers of Urban and Rural area.
2. To compare their intelligence, socio-economic status, attitude towards teaching profession and adjustment.
3. To find out the relationship between teacher effectiveness and

4. To determine the combined effect of the correlates on teacher effectiveness.

The sample comprised 330 teachers of Urban and Rural areas from 22 intermediate colleges of Varanasi, Gorekhpur and Jaunpur districts. The tools used were teacher attitude inventory. Teacher adjustment inventory, SES Scale, Samoohik, Mansik Yogyata, Prakash (1/61) and teaching effectiveness rating scale.

THE MAJOR FINDINGS

1. No significant difference in the mean scores of male and female teachers in their effectiveness was observed.
2. The difference in the mean intelligence scores of male and female teachers was not significant.
3. It was revealed that the rural female teachers had secured comparatively better scores than the rural male teachers in teacher effectiveness.
4. The difference in the mean scores of urban male and female teachers was found to be non-significant on the SES scale.
5. There was no-significant difference in the mean scores of male and female teachers belonging to rural and urban area in their attitude towards teaching.
6. There was no-significant difference in the mean scores of adjustment of male and female teachers.
7. The scores of male and female teachers in teaching effectiveness appeared to be correlated significantly with only two variables-intelligence and attitudes towards the teaching profession.
8. A low relationship between intelligence and socio-economic status was observed. It was however not significant.
9. The teacher effectiveness scores of rural male and female teachers appeared to significantly relate with intelligence, socio-economic status and adjustment.
10. Intelligence showed a moderate and significant relationship with socio-economic status and adjustment of the urban teachers irrespective of sex.

SUSHILA SINGHAL; Stress in Education Indian Experience, Rawat publication, New Delhi, 2004, pp. 294-334.

THE MAJOR FINDINGS

The personal profiles of teachers are not much important, as most of them show mild to moderate levels of stress and burnout, yet the older and those having higher educational qualifications seem to be more stress prone. Those having higher socio-economic status are more involved with students and feel more responsible, but become less idealistic over the tears. In the regular as well as in special schools, teachers experience different levels of stress. So do the males and females, and the more vs. less experienced teachers. The negative perceptions of work-setting can induce negative feelings in teachers resulting in subsequent stress and burnout. Female teachers tend to perceive the work-setting as more positive than males. The special schoolteachers rate their work load higher; their contacts with students more frequent and intense feel more socially isolated and have more role conflicts. More experienced teachers have fewer interpersonal interactions, yet lower social isolation and fewer conflicts in regular as well as special schools. The work-setting of regular schools emerges as the necessary condition, and the stress as the sufficient condition for the onset of burnout. All teachers experience moderate levels of burnout, indicating something more can activate it to be a matter of concern. Males and females both experience it evenly. Teachers in the middle range of experience are more susceptible to stress and burnout than those with a few years or long experience. The finding of work-setting dimensions explaining a higher percent of variance in burnout is interesting to indicate that neither stress is independent of work context, nor all stress gets converted into burnout. Absence of adequate interpersonal interactions and positive feedback, bureaucratic hindrances, greater role conflicts, and difficult and problematic students are good predictors of burnout. Lack of proper training is a good predictor of burnout in special school teachers. The work overload, inadequate orientation few interpersonal interactions, and more role conflicts are associated with greater self-interest. Higher social isolation leads to reduced work goals. Those facing more role conflicts tend to become emotionally detached. The improvements in work-setting need to be initiated to suit the needs of the teachers so that they can efficaciously deliver instruction to their pupils and derive satisfaction from their performance.

❐

18

Methods of Investigation

The present study is titled "A study of the Factors Influencing Teachers Stress among the School Teachers in Chittoor".

NEED FOR THE STUDY

Accomplishment of educational goals and the objectives of teaching is possible only with teachers those who are competent in teaching and free from any type of stress. Teacher stress directly or indirectly influences the competency of teachers in teaching. So the teacher who is subjected to stress may not be possible to teach properly which in term competency in teaching.

Theoretically, the teacher stress may be heard to perform teaching in a competent way. But in practice how far teacher stress is influencing on teaching competency and to what extent teacher stress and teaching competency are related-are the questions waiting for answer. Hence, this study has taken up to find out how teacher stress and teaching competency are inter-related to each other in the context of high school education.

The present investigator has surveyed the available researches on teacher stress and teaching competency and presented in chapter-111.

Design is the heart of research. The following aspects have been discussed in detail, which are concerned with the design of the present study. The present chapter is set apart for making a brief discussion of the objectives of the study, the research procedure includes the operational definitions of the different terms used the various hypotheses that were framed for verification in the present study and the rationale of these hypotheses. The selection of sample includes the sampling techniques used, the reasons for selection of a particular sampling technique and the selection of the sample according to different variables. The selection of suitable tool for collection of data and the procedure followed in administering the tool to collect the data required for the present study.

PROBLEM OF THE SUDY

In the view of the previous chapter, the investigator titled the problem in the following manner. *"A study of factors Influencing Teacher's Stress among the School Teachers in Chittoor"*

OBJECTIVES OF THE STUDY

1. To test the teacher stress and teaching competency scales to be use by the teacher himself.
2. To find out the relationship between teacher stress and teaching competency.
3. To find out the effect of demographical variables in respect of teacher stress.
4. To find out the effect of demographical variables in respect of teaching competency.

ITEM ANALYSIS

For the purpose of determining the degree to which each item is effective in discriminating between high and low teaching competency and item analysis of the data obtained from above sample is undertaken by taking two extreme groups (High and Low) All the fifty two responses of the 200 subjects are scored and scores are arranged in an order from highest score to lowest score. Then the upper 27 per cent of the responses and lower 27per cent of the responses are taken into consideration for measuring significance of difference of means to know the item validity. A.M.S. and S.D.S for the 46 items of upper half and lower half are calculated for all the 46 items between upper and lower half using the following formula.

If the value of the critical ratio 0 the item is greater than 1. 96 (significant at 0.05 level of significant). Then the item is found valid and accepted. If the value of critical ratio of item is less than 1.96 then the item is found invalid and rejected.

RE-TESTING OF TEACHER STRESS SCALE

In the present study, the investigator adopted the Rama's teacher stress self-rating five-point scale developed and standardized by. Dr. Krishnan Raju (1994) because it is more appropriate to measure the teacher stress related to the areas of 1.Professional growth, 2. Work load 3). Occupational Hazards 4).Student behavior 5). Family 6), Societal

The present investigator re-tested this scale on a tryout sample of 200teachers to minimize the error in the tool.

There are 46 items under six different areas of teacher stress scale of Dr. Krishnan Raju. The distribution or 52 items is as fallows. The items are given in appendix-2.

1. Items under professional growth area of teacher stress are 8 i.e., from 1to 8.
2. Items under workload area of teacher stress are 9 i.e., from 9 to 17.
3. Items under occupational Hazards area are of teacher stress are 9 i.e., 18 to26.
4. Items under student behavior area of teacher stress are 9 i.e., 27 to 35.
5. Items under family area of teacher stress are 8 i.e., 36 to43.
6. Items under society area of teacher stress are 3 i.e., 3.

TABLE. 18.1: Showing the Number of Items and Percentage of Items in Teachers Stress.

	Professional Growth	**Work Load**	**Occupational Hazards**	**Student Behavior**	**Family**	**Societal**	**Total**
No.of Que %	8 16.9	9 15.2	9 16.9	9 .9	8 16.9	3 16.9	**46** **99.7**

ADMINISRRATION

This tool I administered to a try out samples of 200 teachers of Chittoor. Instructions to the teachers are given on the title page of the scale. Care is taken to reduce bias in rating. This is done by clearly stating the purpose of study.

SCORING

The responses are scored according to the key. The scoring procedure, which was followed in the teacher competency scale, is followed to this teacher stress also. Total number of items is 46. The maximum is 230 and the minimum possible score is 46 the high score indicates high teacher stress; the low score indicates low teacher stress.

ITEM ANALYSIS

For the purpose of determining the degree to which each item is effective in discriminating high, low stress of teacher an item analysis of the data obtained from the above sample is under taken by taking two extreme groups (High and low) All the 46 responses of the 200subjects are scored and total scores are arranged in an order from highest score to lowest score. Then the upper 27per cent of the total response and lower 27 per cent of total responses are taken into consideration. For measuring significance of the items retained after item analysis for the final student in teacher difference of means to know item validity A.M.S and SDS for all the 46 items of the upper half and lower half are calculated. Critical ratio is then calculated for all the items between upper and lower halves. If the value of critical for ratio of the items is greater than 1.96 (significant at 0.05 level of significance). Then the item is found valid and accepted. If the value of the critical ratio of the item is less than 1.96 then the item is found as invalid and rejected. The scale with all the accepted items used for final study is given in appendix 4.

COLLECTION OF DATA

After retesting the two tools of the study, fresh and final scales are prepared for the final study with personal data pose. There two standardized tools of the resent study are administered to 200teacher of different schools in Chittioor of A.P. for collecting the data the investigator visited each school and administered the scales to the teachers personally. They are advised to put their name, sex, qualification, designation, experience etc. against the place provided in the personal data sheet of each scale.

Instructions are given in the first page of each scale. The investigator requested the teacher to fallow the instruction while responding the tools. Most of the teachers filled the tools on the spot and returned to the investigator. These two tools collected and scored according to the scoring procedure explained in the development and standardization of tools.

SAMPLE

The sample selected for the present investigation consist 200 teachers of different Schools in Chittoor of A.P. The age of the teachers up to 35 and above 35 years, both male and female teachers are found in the sample. Teachers having 2 slabs experience i.e. above15 years, below 15 years are found in the sample. Teachers of two cadres of P.G. and graduate teachers. Another sample Government teacher. Thus, it is found to be a satisfactory sample and the sample is believed to be adequate to test the hypothesis. The sample distribution of the study is shown in below

AGE IN YEARS	ABOVE 35	BELOW 35
	121	79
SEX	MALE	FEMALE
	88	112
GENERAL QUALIFICATION	GRADUATES	P.G
	100	100
TEACHING EXPERIENCE	ABOVE 35	BELOW 35
	84	116
MANAGEMENT	GOVT.	PRIVATE
	99	101

ANALYSIS OF DATA

The following statistical techniques are used to analyze the data.

1. Mean and standard deviations of all the distributions are calculated.
2. To find out the relationship between teaching competency and Teacher stress "r" values are computed.
3. Co-efficiency of co-relation for the entire dimension was also calculated.
4. Critical ratios are calculated for testing the subsidiary hypothesis.

HYPOTHESES OF THE STUDY

1. There is no significant difference between Above 35 years age of teachers and Below 35 years age of teacher towards teacher stress.
2. There is no significant difference between Male and Female teachers towards teacher stress.
3. There is no significant difference between Graduate teachers and post Graduate Teachers towards teacher stress.

4. There is no significant difference between Above 15 tears, and Below 15 years teaching experience towards teacher stress.
5. There is no significant difference between Government School Teachers and Private school Teachers towards teacher stress.
6. There is no significant difference between Male and Female Teachers towards teacher stress in Professional growth.
7. There is no significant difference between Male and Female Teachers towards teacher stress in Work Load.
8. There is no significant difference between Male and Female Teachers towards teacher stress in Occupational Hazards.
9. There is no significant difference between Male and Female Teachers towards teacher stress in Student Behaviour.
10. There is no significant difference between Male and Female Teachers towards teacher stress in Family.
11. There is no significant difference between Graduate teachers and Post Graduate Teachers towards teacher stress in Professional Growth
12. There is no significant difference between Graduate teachers and Post Graduate Teachers towards teacher stress in Work Load
13. There is no significant difference between Graduate teachers and Post Graduate Teachers towards teacher stress in Occupational Hazards.
14. There is no significant difference between Graduate teachers and Post Graduate Teachers towards teacher stress in Student Behaviour
15. There is no significant difference between Graduate teachers and Post Graduate Teachers towards teacher stress in Family.

LIMITATIONS OF THE STUDY

1. The study is limited to only teachers of different primary and secondary schools in Chittoor of A.P.
2. Of the three criteria of teaching competency, only two criteria i.e. presage and process are covered in this study.
3. To measure the teaching competency and teacher stress teacher self – rating scales are used in this study.
4. Of many dimensions of teaching competency, planning presentation, closing evaluation, and managerial dimensions are considered in this study.
5. Of many dimensions of teacher stress professional growth, work load, Occupational hazards, Students behavior, family and societal dimensions are considered in this study

PROCEDURE

In order to test the Hypothesis the investigator planned and executed in three steps

1. Measurement of teacher stress with the help of standardized teacher stress,
2. Measurement of teaching competency with the help of Rama's teaching competency scale.
3. Using appropriate statistical procedures to find out relationship between teacher stress and teaching competency.

RE-TESTING OF RAMA'S TEACHER STRESS SCALE

In the present study, the investigator adopted the Rama's teacher stress self rating five point scale developed and standardized by Prof. R. Rama (2004) because it is more appropriate to measure the teacher stress related to the areas of

1. **Professional Growth 2. Workload 3. Occupational Hazards 4. Student Behavior 5. Family 6. Societal.**
    1. There are 46 items under 6 different areas of teacher stress scale of Prof. R. Rama.
    2. Items under professional growth area of teacher stress are 8 i.e., from 1to 8.
    3. Items under Work Load area of teacher stress are 9 i.e., from 9 to 17.
    4. Items under Occupational Hazards area of teacher stress are 9 i.e., from18 to 26.
    5. Items under Student Behavior area of teacher stress are 9 i.e., from 27 to 35.
    6. Items under Family area of teacher stress are 8 i.e., from 36 to 43.
    7. Items under Societal area of teacher stress are 3 i.e., from 44 to 46.

TABLE. 18.2: Variable wise Distribution of the Sample

Variable	Categories	Size	Grand Total
Sex	Male	85	200
	Female	115	
Age	Above 35	129	200
	Below 35	71	
Qualification	Graduate	92	200
	Post-Graduate	108	

Management	Government	99	200
	Private	101	
Teaching Experience	Above 15	92	200
	Below 15	108	

SELECTION OF THE TOOL

A research tool plays a major role in any worthwhile research as it is the sole factor is determining the sound data and in arriving at perfect conclusions about the problem or study on hand, which ultimately, helps in providing suitable remedial measures to the problem concerned.

The progress of making depends upon well-conducted research programme. Well conducted research programmes postulate sufficient, reliable and valid facts such facts are obtained through a systematic procedure, which involves various devices. Each rehear tool is appropriate in a given situation to accomplish a particular purpose. It may be stressed that these tools may be used in combination. They supplement the work of each other.

John Best observes, "Like the tools in the carpenter box, each research tool is appropriate in a given situation to accomplish a particular purpose". Each data gathering –device has both merits and Hazards of limitations.

Different tools are used to collect various kinds of information for different purposes. The investigator should familiarize themselves with nature, merits and limitations of these tools and should attempt to learn how to construct and use them effectively.

The following are some of the tools generally employed for the purpose of research.

a. Inquiry forms:

1. Questionnaire
2. Schedule
3. Check-list
4. Rating scale
5. Score card
6. Attitude scale

b. Observation

c. Interview

d. Sociometry

e. Psychological tests:

1. Achivement test
2. Aptitude test
3. Intelligence test
4. Interest Inventory
5. Personality measures

Inequity forms are class of data gathering devices which make use of properly prepared Performa or forms for enquiring into and securing information about certain phenomena under study. Out of number of such inequity forms, perhaps the most used and the most abused of tools is the questionnaire.

Keeping in view the desirability and suitability for the collection of the data, the investigator adapted the questionnaire in case of the present investigation.

ADMINISTRATION OF THE TOOL

The investigator personally went to each institution and has taken permission from the respective head of the institutions and personally administered to 200 teachers in the various schools. The investigator first explained to the teachers about the importance of the investigation and attitude of teachers towards teacher stress in relation to teaching competency in school teachers. As stated earlier, the present investigation is intended to the attitudes of schoolteachers.

ANALISIS OF THE DATA

The following statistical techniques are followed to analyze of the data.

1. Mean and Standard Deviation of all the distributions are calculated.
2. To find out the relationship between teacher stress and teaching competency 'r' values are computed.

The analyze and interpretation of the present data is presented in proceeding Chapter

SCORING PROCEDURE

The responses are scored in stress according to key, for all the items scores from five to one for the five responses i.e. N. S. (No stress), Mi. S (Mild stress), Mo. S (Moderate Stress), M. S.(More Stress), S. S. (Sevier Stress) total No. of items 46 in teacher stress scale.

TABLE.18.3: The Weightage given to Responses

Kind of Responses	Marks
No Stress (N.S)	5
Mild Stress (Mi. S.)	4
Moderate Stress (Mo. S.)	3
More Stress (M. S.)	2
Sevier Stress (S. S.)	1

STITISTICAL TECHNIQUES USED

The above-mentioned hypotheses, which were framed keeping the variables like age, sex, teaching experience, medium of teaching, Qualification Type of management were taken into consideration. The collected data analyzed and the results are interpreted and statistical aspects like means, standard deviation and critical ratios are taken as the statistical techniques to study and analyze the variables. Co-efficient of co-relation with the help of scatter diagram was made use of to study the reliability of the test scores. The technique of the significance of the difference between means is used. Here technique only large samples in different categories considered for comparison so that use was made only of the formula for large samples. It was further assumed that the means were uncorrelated. Where,

A.M = Arithmetic mean

A.A.M = Assumed arithmetic mean

S.D = Standard deviation

C.R = Critical Ratio

1,2 = Standard deviation of two samples

M_1, m_2 = Means of the two samples

N_1,N_2 = The size of the two sample

❒

19

Analysis and Interpretation of the Data

Data analysis is the heart of any social science research. Using questionnaire or any inventory the researcher collects the information. Until and unless, it is proposed through statistical treatment, it serves no purpose. The researcher using the standardized procedure that tool so constructed collected data from various variables. The he collected information is given numerical scoring and scores are tabulated. The mean, median, mode, quartile deviation, standard deviation, kurtosis etc. are also obtained. Basing on the responses of the individuals the researcher tabulated the item of the tool according to their scoring order presented findings and calculations. Finally, the researcher presented suggestions for the teacher stress in relation to teaching competency scope for further research.

ANALYSIS

The analysis and interpretation of data involves the objectives material in the processions of the research and his subjective and desires to derive from the data, the inherent meaning in their relation to the problem. To avoid making conclusions are interpretations from insufficient are invalid data, the final analysis must be anticipated in detailed when plans are being made for collecting information.

J. C. Agarwal, has explained thus:"However values, reliable and adequate the data may be, it does not serve any worthwhile purpose unless it is carefully edited. Systematically analyzed intelligently interpreted and rationally concluded".

Analysis of data means studying the tabulated material in order to determine inherent facts of meaning. It involves breaking down existing complex factors into smaller parts and putting the together in new arrangements for purposes interpretation.

THE FOLLOWING ARE THE METHODS MOST COMMONLY USED IN STATISTICAL ANALYSIS

1. Calculating frequency distribution (usually in percentage) of items under study.
2. Testing the data for morality of distribution-Skewness and Kurtosis.
3. Calculating methods of central tendency –Mean, Median, Mode and establishing norms.
4. Calculating percentile and percentile ranks.
5. Calculating measures of dispersion –Standard deviation, Mean deviation, Quartile deviation and Range.
6. Calculating measures of relationship-Coefficient of correlation reliability and validity.
7. Graphical representation of data –Frequency Polygon curve, Hectograph, Cumulative frequency, Polygon and Ogive etc.

In the process of analysis of the data, the investigators usually make used of us many of the above simply statistical devises as necessary for purpose of their study. There are some other complicated devices of statistical analysis which researches use in particular experimental or complex casual comparative studies investigation.

INTERPRETATION

"The process of interpretation is essentially one of the stating what the results (findings) show, what do they means What is their significance What is the answer to original problem Interpretation is thus by no means a much of process. Its uses of scientific examination of the results of one's analysis in the light of all the limitations of the data gathering, Interpretation means the application of deductive and inductive logic to the research process.

Interpretation is the most important step in the total procedure of research, it is purely subjective and many errors are made at their stage. An adequate knowledge not only of techniques of research, but also of one's field of study and a capacity to do carefully and critical thinking are very essential to safe guard against misinterpretation of facts collected.

The analysis and interpretation of the data represent the application of deductive and inductive logic to the research process. Interpretation calls for a critical examination of the result of one's analysis in the light of all the limitation of the data gathering and his subjective attitude to avoid subjectively, one must be critical on one's own thinking.

Good, Barr and Scats the following characteristics of good generalizations.

1. Education generalization should be conceivable and in agreement with facts.
2. They should not conflict with the known laws of nature of previously established generalization.
3. They should be stated in the simplest possible terms.
4. They should be amenable to deductive reasoning.

In this part the result of present study are analyzed and interpreted. The results are presented and all the hypotheses are tested and verified in the present study, the results are analyzed and presented in three parts.

1. The first part deals with related to significant relationship between the teacher stress and teaching competency.
2. The second part deals with testing the hypotheses pertaining to teacher stress.
3. The third part deals with testing the hypotheses pertaining to teaching competency.

TESTING OF HYPOTHESES-1

There is no significant difference between above 35 years age of teachers and blow 35 years age of teachers towards teachers stress.

To test the validity of the above hypothesis, the following calculations are made. Table showing the significant difference between above 35 years age of teachers and below 35 years age of teacher in respect of teachers stress.

TABLE. 19.1

Age	N	Mean	SD	't' Value
1.00 2.00	129 71	161.66 158.87	35.70 29.49	0.56 @

From the above table the calculated 't' value is 0.56 found to be less than the table value (1.96) at 0.05 level. Hence, the hypothesis-1 is accepted. Hence, there is no significance difference between above 35 years age of teachers and below 35 years age of teachers towards teacher stress.

TESTING OF HYPOTHESES - 2

There is no significant difference between male and female teachers towards teacher stress. To test the validity of the above hypothesis, the following calculations are made. The table showing the significant differences between male and female teachers in respect of teacher stress.

TABLE. 19.2

Sex	N	Mean	SD	't' Value
1.00 2.00	85 115	28.41 29.78	6.02 6.33	1.54 @

From the above table the calculated 't' value is 1.54 found to be less than the table value (1.96) at 0.05 level. Hence, the hypothesis-2 is accepted. Hence, there is no significance difference between male and female teacher towards teacher stress.

TESTING OF HYPOTHESES - 3

There is no significant difference between graduate teachers and post-graduate teachers towards teacher stress. To test the validity of the above hypothesis, the following calculations are made. The table showing the significant differences between graduate teachers and post-graduate teachers in respect of teacher stress.

TABLE. 19.3

Educational Qualification	N	Mean	SD	't' Value
1.00 2.00	92 108	164.22 157.63	37.00 30.20	1.386 @

From the above table the calculated 't' value is 1.386 found to be greater than the table value (1.96) at 0.05 level. Hence, the hypothesis-3 is accepted. Hence, there no is significance difference between graduate teacher and post-graduate teachers towards teacher stress.

TESTING OF HYPOTHESES - 6

There is no significant difference between male and female teachers towards teacher stress in professional growth.

To test the validity of the above hypothesis, the following calculations are made. The table showing the significant differences between male and female teachers in respect of teacher stress in professional growth.

TABLE. 19.4

Sex	N	Mean	SD	't' Value
1.00 2.00	85 115	28.41 29.78	6.02 6.33	01.544 @

From the above table the calculated 't' value is 01.544 found to be less than the table value (1.96) at 0.05 level. Hence, the hypothesis-6 is accepted. Hence, there is no significance difference between male and female teacher towards teacher stress in professional growth.

TESTING OF HYPOTHESES - 7

There is no significant difference between male and female teachers towards teacher stress in work load.

To test the validity of the above hypothesis, the following calculations are made. The table showing the significant differences between male and female teachers in respect of teacher stress in work load.

TABLE. 19.5

Sex	N	Mean	SD	't' Value
1.00 2.00	85 115	30.20 31.32	8.22 8.44	0.939 @

From the above table the calculated't' value is -.939 found to be greater than the table value (1.96) at 0.05 level. Hence, the hypothesis-7 is accepted. Hence, there is no significance difference between male and female teacher towards teacher stress in workload.

TESTING OF HYPOTHESES - 8

There is no significant difference between male and female teachers towards teacher stress in occupational hazards.

To test the validity of the above hypothesis, the following calculations are made. The table showing the significant differences between male and female teachers in respect of teacher stress in occupational hazards.

TABLE. 19.6

Sex	N	Mean	SD	't' Value
1.00 2.00	85 115	31.44 32.20	7.34 7.91	0.685 @

From the above table the calculated 't' value is 0.685 found to be greater than the table value (1.96) at 0.05 level. Hence, the hypothesis-8 is accepted. Hence, there is no significance difference between male and female teacher towards teacher stress in occupational hazards.

TESTING OF HYPOTHESES - 9

There is no significant difference between male and female teachers towards teacher stress in student behaviour.

To test the validity of the above hypothesis, the following calculations are made. The table showing the significant differences between male and female teachers in respect of teacher stress in student behaviour.

TABLE. 19.7

Sex	N	Mean	SD	't' Value
1.00	85	30.87	8.51	1.386
2.00	115	29.26	7.81	@

From the above table the calculated 't' value is 1.386 found to be greater than the table value (1.96) at 0.05 level. Hence, the hypothesis-9 is accepted. Hence, there is no significance difference between male and female teacher towards teacher stress in student behaviour.

TESTING OF HYPOTHESES - 10

There is no significant difference between male and female teachers towards teacher stress in family.

To test the validity of the above hypothesis, the following calculations are made. The table showing the significant differences between male and female teachers in respect of teacher stress in family.

TABLE. 19.8

Sex	N	Mean	SD	't' Value
1.00	85	28.01	7.266	1.305
2.00	115	29.417	7.72	@

From the above table the calculated 't' value is 1.305 found to be greater than the table value (1.96) at 0.05 level. Hence, the hypothesis-10 is accepted. Hence, there is no significance difference between male and female teacher towards teacher stress in family.

TESTING OF HYPOTHESES - 11

There is no significant difference between graduate teachers and post-graduate teachers towards stress in professional growth.

To test the validity of the above hypothesis, the following calculations are made. The table showing the significant differences between graduate teachers and post-graduate teachers in respect of teacher stress in professional growth.

TABLE. 19.9

Educational Qualification	N	Mean	SD	't' Value
1.00 2.00	92 108	29.81 28.67	6.70 5.77	1.291 @

From the above table the calculated 't' value is 1.291 found to be greater than the table value (1.96) at 0.05 level. Hence, the hypothesis-11 is accepted. Hence, there is no significance difference between graduate teacher and post-graduate teachers towards teacher stress in professional growth.

TESTING OF HYPOTHESES - 12

There is no significant difference between graduate teachers and post-graduate teachers towards stress in workload.

To test the validity of the above hypothesis, the following calculations are made. The table showing the significant differences between graduate teachers and post-graduate teachers in respect of teacher stress in workload.

TABLE. 19.10

Educational Qualification	N	Mean	SD	't' Value
1.00 2.00	92 108	32.4348 29.4907	8.3827 8.1166	2.518 *

From the above table the calculated 't' value is 2.518 found to be less than the table value (1.96) at 0.05 level. Hence, the hypothesis-12 is rejected. Hence, there is significance difference between graduate teacher and post-graduate teachers towards teacher stress in workload.

TESTING OF HYPOTHESES - 14

There is no significant difference between graduate teachers and post-graduate teachers towards stress in student behaviour.

To test the validity of the above hypothesis, the following calculations are made. The table showing the significant differences between graduate teachers and post-graduate teachers in respect of teacher stress in student behaviour.

TABLE. 19.11

Educational Qualification	N	Mean	SD	't' Value
1.00 2.00	92 108	30.0109 29.8889	8.7549 7.6162	0.105 @

From the above table the calculated 't' value is 0.105 found to be greater than the table value (1.96) at 0.05 level. Hence, the hypothesis-14 is accepted. Hence, there is no significance difference between graduate teacher and post-graduate teachers towards teacher stress in student behaviour.

TESTING OF HYPOTHESES - 15

There is no significant difference between graduate teachers and post-graduate teachers towards stress in family.

To test the validity of the above hypothesis, the following calculations are made. The table showing the significant differences between graduate teachers and post-graduate teachers in respect of teacher stress in family.

TABLE. 19.12

Educational Qualification	N	Mean	SD	't' Value
1.00	92	29.27	7.68	0.781
2.00	108	28.43	7.44	@

From the above table the calculated 't' value is 0.781 found to be greater than the table value (1.96) at 0.05 level. Hence, the hypothesis-15 is accepted. Hence, there is no significance difference between graduate teacher and post-graduate teachers towards teacher stress in family.

❐

20

Summary and Conclusion

It is high time to identify the problem of the teacher in particular his competency and his mental agony to make the teaching learning process useful to the present day condition. In the modern days teacher is loaded with so many sophisticated technological trends that were place in the modern human beings also confronted with many perplexing problems caused due to perpetually changing world resulting in frustration, Conflict, Anxiety, Stress and so on. Coleman in n1982 also observed that, "The 17th century has been called the age of enlightenment, the 18th century the age of reason, the 19th century the age of progress and the 20th century the age of anxiety". This emphasizes that a meaningful and satisfying way of life has become difficult in this age of anxiety the teacher of today is not exempted from the above age of anxiety.

Teaching is a sensitive weapon to achieve the expected educational goals through effective teaching learning process. The effective teaching is possible only with the teacher, those who are mentally sound. We should make the teacher away from the Anxiety, Stress and so on. So as to utilize all his teaching competencies to make the teaching learning processes in an effective way.

The modern research studies observed that the teacher performance and teacher behaviour are strongly affected by stress. ARYACDU and SUTCLIFFE (1977) stated that," The stress with the teaching profession may affect the school as an organization, teacher performance, the physical and emotional well being of the teacher".

The modern research studies observed that the teacher performance and teacher behaviour are strongly affected by stress. ARYACDU and SUTCLIFRE (1977) stated the, "The stress with the teaching profession may affect the school as an organization, teacher performance, the physical and emotional well being of the teacher".

MEANING OF STRESS

Stress is a condition stream on one's emotions, thought processes and physical conditions. When it is excessive, it can pretend once ability to cope with environment. (Hans Selye, 1976) "Stress is the general term applied to the pressures; employs developed various symptoms of stress as, "an adjective demand placed on the organism".

Stress has been defined following Lazarus's model, as a state of imbalance when the demands made on the person in different areas of life exceed her / his capabilities and resources (Lazarus and Folkman , 1984)

Stress has been defined following Lazarus (1974) as a state arising from imbalance between the demands made and the coping resources at one's disposal.

Stress has been defined as a state of imbalance between one's personal resources and the environmental demands, and manifested in the form of a number of psychosomatic factor, such as Somatization, Obsessive-Compulsive interpersonal sensitivity, Depression and Anxiety.

TEACHER STRESS

Job stress is most common psychological phenomena that is prevalent among people who are in different jobs and professions. The stress studies are initially directed toward industrial organizations within the private sector. Researchers have come to believe that stress may be especially prevalent among human service profession, particularly the teaching profession, (Kjyiacou and Suteliffe 1977-78; Pettegrew and Wolf 1982, Cherniss 1980: and Coorper and Marshall 1980). As a teaching is a human service profession, stress within the teaching profession is considerable and may have far-reaching consequences on the entire education system. Teaching is complex process were in teacher is expected to exhibit many skills. This makes a teacher to experiences stress in the profession.

Further, Pettergrew and Wolf (1982) opined that 'Teacher stress has a nationwide concern and relatively new area of empirical research".

Factors prepared by teachers as being troublesome or stressful have included students discipline, negative attitudes towards school, physical violence, is adequate preparation time, lack of clear role definition and heavy workloads". (Bearly, Myette and Serma, 1983; Chichen and Koff, 1978; Olander and Ferrel, 1970).

Teacher is subjected to stress due to incoherent social life, widening social distance, segregation, lack of societal support, corruption, nepotism, unnecessary societal involvement in day-to-day activities, high degree of social indiscipline, deterioration of values, lack of social security etc.

EFFECTS OF TEACHER STRESS

As job stress effect organizational performance, teacher stress impedes teacher performance in teaching. Infect it is assumed that mild stress can even enhance performance but high level of stress can create physical, Psychological and behavioural problems among teacher. There are several research studies, which observed that, a high level of stress accompanied by physical illness such as high blood pressures, ulcers and even cancer. Similarly high level of stress may be accompanied by psychological problems such as anger, anxiety, depression, nervousness, irritability, tension and boredom. Excessive stress may also result in behavioural problems such as sleeplessness, under eating or over eating, increased smoking and drinking and drug abuse. Many researches of teacher

TEACHER COMPETENCY AND STRESS-A BRIEFOUTLINE

The study is about teacher competency in relation to stress. Teacher competence, in general scene, impedes when teacher suffer from stress. In this chapter, a discussion is made about teacher competency, stress, and the development of this type of study in the world.

"Teacher competency" refers to the set of knowledge, abilities and beliefs a teacher possess and bring to the teaching situation. Teacher competence differs from teacher performance and teacher effectiveness in that it is a stable characteristic of the teacher that does not change appreciably when the teacher moves from one situation to another. It resembles teacher performance in that it has also been proposed as a basis from which teach effectiveness can be inferred.

NEED FOR THE STUDY

Accomplishment of educational goals and the objectives of teaching is possible only with the teacher those who are competent in teaching and free from any type of stress. Teacher stress directly or indirectly influences the competency of teacher in teaching. So the teacher who is subjected to stress may not be possible to teach properly which in term Indus is competency in teaching. Theoretically, this teacher stress may be heard to perform teaching in a competent way. But in practice how for teacher stress is influencing on teaching competency and to what extent teacher stress and teaching competency are related-are the questions waiting for answer. Hence, this study has taken up to find out how teacher stress teaching competency are inter related to each other in the context of high school education.

OBJECTIVES OF THE STUDY

1. To test the teacher stress and teaching competency scales to be use by the teacher himself.
2. To find out the relationship between teacher stress and teaching competency.
3. To find out the effect of demographical variables in respect of teacher stress.
4. To find out the effect of demographical variables in respect of teaching competency.

HYPOTHESES OF THE STUDY

1. There is no significant difference between Above 35 years age of teachers and Below 35 years age of teachers towards teacher stress.
2. There is no significant difference between Male and Female Teachers towards teacher stress.
3. There is no significant difference between Graduate teachers and Post Graduate Teachers towards teacher stress.
4. There is no significant difference between Above 15 tears, and Below 15 years teaching experience towards teacher stress.
5. There is no significant difference between Government School Teachers and Private school Teachers towards teacher stress.
6. There is no significant difference between Male and Female Teachers towards teacher stress in Professional growth.
7. There is no significant difference between Male and Female Teachers towards teacher stress in Work Load.
8. There is no significant difference between Male and Female Teachers towards teacher stress in Occupational Hazards.
9. There is no significant difference between Male and Female Teachers towards teacher stress in Student Behaviour.
10. There is no significant difference between Male and Female Teachers towards teacher stress in Family.
11. There is no significant difference between Graduate teachers and Post Graduate Teachers towards teacher stress in Professional Growth
12. There is no significant difference between Graduate teachers and Post Graduate Teachers towards teacher stress in Work Load

13. There is no significant difference between Graduate teachers and Post Graduate Teachers towards teacher stress in Occupational Hazards.
14. There is no significant difference between Graduate teachers and Post Graduate Teachers towards teacher stress in Student Behaviour
15. There is no significant difference between Graduate teachers and Post Graduate Teachers towards teacher stress in Family.

LIMITATIONS OF THE STUDY

1. The study is limited to only teachers of different schools in Chittoor of A.P.
2. Of the three criteria of teaching competency, only two criteria i.e. presage and process are covered in this study.
3. To measure the teaching competency and teacher stress teacher self – rating scales are used in this study.
4. Of many dimensions of teaching competency, planning presentation, closing evaluation, and managerial dimensions are considered in this study.
5. Of many dimensions of teacher stress professional growth, work load, Occupational hazards, Students behavior, family and societal dimensions are considered in this study

CONCLUSIONS

From the present study only one factor that is Educational Qualification as significant impact on teachers stress. The male teachers Mean value is 32.4348, which is more than Female teachers mean value (29.4907). The other factors are viz.,

1. There is no significance difference between Above 35 year's age of teachers and below 35 years age of teachers towards teacher stress.
2. There is no significance difference between Male and Female teachers towards teacher stress.
3. There is no significance difference between Graduate teachers and Post-Graduate teachers towards teacher stress.
4. There is no significance difference between Experience of above 15 years and below 15 years towards teacher stress.
5. There is no significance difference between Govt. school teachers and private school teachers towards teacher stress.
6. There is no significance difference between Male and Female teachers towards teacher stress in professional growth.
7. There is no significance difference between Male and Female teachers towards teacher stress in Work Load.

8. There is no significance difference between Male and Female teachers towards teacher stress in Occupational Hazards.
9. There is no significance difference between Male and Female teachers towards teacher stress in Student behaviour.
10. There is no significance difference between Male and Female teachers towards teacher stress in Family.
11. There is no significance difference between Graduate teachers and Post-Graduate teachers towards teacher stress in Professional Growth.
12. There is significance difference between Graduate teachers and Post-Graduate teachers towards teacher stress in Work Load.
13. There is no significance difference between Graduate teachers and Post-Graduate teachers towards teacher stress in Occupational Hazards.
14. There is no significance difference between Graduate teachers and Post-Graduate teachers towards teacher stress in Student behaviour.
15. There is no significance difference between Graduate teachers and Post-Graduate teachers towards teacher stress in Family.
16. Hence, there is no significant impact on teachers stress. Teachers would give more importance for the quality of education. It is necessary to encourage teachers to study for the further education. The role of Government is also important to motivate the teachers towards higher education.

SUGGESTIONS

Exercise: Physical exercise is accepted as the best antidote to stress. It keeps the body healthy, makes one emotionally strong, and eases nervous tension. It keeps the mind, body and action coordinated.

Relaxation: Relaxation response is an innate physiological change elicited by some psychological means. Evidence indicates that the immune function in the body improves by relaxation training, and its regular practice can help maintain the cool. These can include hobbies like reading, listening to music, etc.

Value Education: Intervention for change in social and practical values can help them think and act rationally and proactively.

Meditation: It is a continuous scream of effortless concentration, on a single point, over an extended period. It is suggested that the concentration should be maintained unbroken. Psychologists have argued that meditation leads to better emotional and physical health.

Yoga: A stress management programme in the Indian setting may combine some elements of Gita and Yoga in the preventive plans. Srivastava (1981) concluded that persons coping more effectively with stress have more positive orientation to life in general, and employ a valuable mix of coping and defence response. Yoga is a holistic science, which gives to the person tools and techniques to expand conscious awareness into the unconscious In order to become aware of the patterns and tendencies that cause stress.

1. It is to be suggested that teachers effects teaching competency.
2. The stress creators harm the teacher effectiveness and teaching competency
3. The government or Private management of the institution should improve the conditions for better teaching by reducing the stress factors.
4. The main stress creators like lack of promotional opportunities lack of professional growth are to be tackled to improve the teaching competency.
5. Unless stress creators are reduced qualitative improvement teaching, learning process cannot be improved.

SUGGESTIONS FOR FURTHER STUDY

1. The study may be extended to higher and primary education.
2. To measure the teaching competency presage, process and product variables may be compared.
3. Stress and psychological well-being Among Tribal and Non-Tribal primary school teachers.
4. Stress and burnout among teachers in Regular and special schools.
5. Stress and coping among college students.
6. Stress and Coping among Adolescents.
7. Relationship between teaching competency and teacher motivation may be studied.
8. Relationship between teacher stress and teacher adjustment may be studied.
9. An extensive study is needed for teacher stress and teaching competency.

❐

Bibliography

1. Beck, J. Gayle; McNiff, Judiann; Clapp, Joshua D.; Olsen, Shira A.; Avery, Carlo, Gustavo; McGinley,Meredith; Davis, Alexandra; Streit, CaraChow, Pizza Ka-Yee; Cheng, Sheung-Tak *Journal of Counseling Psychology,*v57n1 p.92-104 Jan 2010 and Purpose. Islam&Science, 1(1).
2. De Hoyos, Librado R.; Ramirez, Noe *Journal of Ethnic & Cultural Diversity in Social Work,* v15 n1-2 p.147-166 2006http://www.tandf.co.uk/journals
3. Diener, E., Emmons, R.A., Larson, R.J., & Griffin, S. (1985). The satisfaction with life scale. Journal of Personality Assessment, 49, 71-75.
4. Dordrecht, Netherlands: Springer, 2005. Phenomenology of Life: Meating the Challanges of the Present Day World (Analecta Husserliana: The Year Book of Phenomenological Research. Vol. LXXXIV)
5. Efthim, Paul W.; Kenny, Maureen E.; Mahalik, James R. *Journal of Counselling & Development,* v79 n4 p.430-38 Fall 2001
6. Faiver, Christopher M.; O'Brien, Eugene M.; Ingersoll, R. Elliott *Journal of Counselling & Development,* v78 n2 p.55-61 Sep 2000
7. Ferguson, Tamara J.; Stegge, Hedy; Miller, Erin R.; Olsen, Michael E. *Developmental Psychology,* v35 n2 p.47-57 Mar 1999
8. Golshani, Mehdi, 2003. Does Science Offer Evidence of a Transcendent Reality?
9. Grünberg, David, (A) "The Meaning of Life Vis-A-Vis the Challenges of the Present Day World," in Anna-Teresa Tymieniecka (ed.),

10. Grünberg, David, (B) 2005. Etik ve Ya"amın Anlamı, Erdem, 44.
11. Guastello, Stephen, Chaos, Catastrophe, and Human Affairs: Applications of Nonlinear Dynamics to Work, Organizations, and Social Evolution, Lawrence Erlbaum Associates, Mahwah, NJ, 1995.
12. Hesse, Herman, Siddartha, New Directions Paper Book, 1957
13. Hursthouse, Rosalind, 2003, "Virtue Ethics", Stanford Encyclopaedia of Philosophy, Edward N. Zalta (ed.), retrieved 6 April, 2010 from http://plato.stanford.edu/entries/ethics-virtue/#2
14. Johnson, Diane Elizabeth *College Student Journal*, v46 n1 p.3-17 Mar 2012
15. Johnson,Veronica R.F.;Yarhouse, Mark A. *Counselling and Values,* v58 n1 p.85-103 Apr 2013
16. Joske, W., D. (2004).Philosophy and the Meaning of Life. In David Benatar (ed.), Life, Death and Meaning: Key Philosophical Readings on the Big Questions (pp. 49– 62). USA, Rowman and Littlefield Publishers Inc. Kraut, Richard, (2001). "Aristotle's Ethics", Stanford Encyclopedia of Philosophy. Retrived August 01, 2010.
17. Kamper, Heidrun Journal of *Multilingual and Multicultural Development,* v25 n5-6 p.497-511, 2004
18. Kamper, Heidrun Journal of *Multilingual and Multicultural Development,* v25 n5-6 p.497-511, 2004 http://www.tandf.co.uk/journals
19. Kim, Jungmeen; Talbot, Nancy L.; Cicchetti, Dante *Child Abuse & Neglect: the International Journal,* v33 n6 p.362-371, Jun 2009
20. Kim, Sangmoon; Thibodeau, Ryan; Jorgensen, Randall S. *Psychological Bulletin,* v137 n1 p.68-96 Jan 2011
21. Kim, Sangmoon; Thibodeau, Ryan; Jorgensen, Randall S. *Psychological Bulletin,* v137 n1 p.68-96 Jan 2011
22. Kolves, Kairi; Ide, Naoko; De Leo, Diego *Suicide and Life-Threatening Behavior,* v41 n2 p.149-159 Apr 2011
23. Konstam, Varda; Chernoff, Miriam; Deveney, Sara *Counselling and Values,* v46 n1 p.26-39 Oct 2001
24. Kristin; Rhea, Deborah J.; Oomen, Jody *American Journal of Health Education,* v35 n3 p.152-157 May-Jun 2004http://www.aahperd.org
25. Luby, Joan; Belden, Andy; Sullivan, Jill; Hayen, Robin; McCadney, Amber; Spitznagel, Ed *Journal of Child Psychology and Psychiatry,* v50 n9 p.1156-1166 Sep 2009
26. Megan L.; Hagewood, J. Houston *Behavior Therapy,* v42 n4 p.740-750 Dec 2011
27. Meyer, Janet R. *Western Journal of Communication,* v77 n2 p.210-230, 2013

28. Mills, R.S.L. *Developmental Review,* v25 n1 p.26-63 Mar 2005
29. *New Directions for Youth Development,* n136 p.75-93 Win 2012
30. Thomaes, Sander; Stegge, Hedy; Olthof, Tjeert *British Journal of Developmental Psychology,* v25 n4 p.559-577 Nov 2007
31. Updike, Thomas L., Jr.; And Others *Psychology: A Quarterly Journal of Human Behavior,* v24 n1-2 p.60-64, 1987
32. Wietzker, Anne; Buysse, Ann *Psychological Assessment*, v24 n3 p.783-789, Sep 2012
33. Wiginton, Kristin; Rhea, Deborah J.; Oomen, Jody *American Journal of Health Education,* v35 n3 p.152-157 May-Jun 2004
34. Wiginton, Kristin; Rhea, Deborah J.; Oomen, Jody *American Journal of Health Education,* v35 n3 p.152-157 May-Jun 2004
35. Williams, Kate; Donaghue, Ngaire; Kurz, Tim *Psychology of Women Quarterly,* v37 n1 p.97-112, Mar 2013
36. Williams, Neil F. *Journal of Physical Education, Recreation & Dance,* v86 n1 p.36-39, 2015
37. Wilson, Tom *Journal of Education & Christian Belief,* v18 n2 p.155-169 2014
38. Andrini, B. & Kagan, S. (1990). Cooperative learning: A multi-structural approach. San Juan Capistrano, CA: Resources for Teachers, Inc.
39. Aronson, E., Blaney, N., Stephan, C., Sikes, J., & Snap, M. (1978) The jigsaw classroom. Sage, Beverly Hills, California, USA.
40. Anderson C (2005) Enabling and shaping understanding through tutorials. In: Marton F, Hounsell D and Entwistle N (eds) The Experience of Learning: Implications for Teaching and Studying in Higher Education, 3rd Internet edition. Edinburgh: Centre for Teaching, Learning and Assessment, University of Edinburgh, pp. 187–97.
41. Antil, L., Jenkins, J., Wayne, S., & Vadsay, P. (1998). Cooperative learning: conceptualizations, and the relation between research and practice. American Educational Research Journal, 35, 419- 454.
42. Ames, C. & Archer, J. (1988). Achievement goals in the classroom: Students' learning strategies and motivation processes. Journal of Educational Psychology, 80, 260–267.
43. Bennett, N., & Cass, J. (1988). The effects of group composition on group interactive processes and pupil understanding. British Educational Research Journal, 15, 19-32.
44. Bondwell, C.C. & Eison, J. A. (1991) Active Learning: Creating Excitement in the Classroom. ASHE - ERIC Higher Education Reports.

45. Bruffee, K. A. (1993). Collaborative learning: Higher education, interdependence, and the authority of knowledge. Baltimore, MD: The Johns Hopkins University Press.
46. Cohen, E. G. (1994). Restructuring the classroom: conditions for productive small groups. Review of Educational Research, 64, 1-35.
47. Cabrera, A. F.; Crissman, J. L.; Bernal, E. M.; Nora, A.; Terenzini, P. T.; Pascarella, E. T. Collaborative Learning: Its Impact on College Students' Development and Diversity. J.Coll. Stud. Development 2002, 43(1), 20–34.
48. Cosden, M., Pearl, R. & Bryan, T.H. (1985).The effects of cooperative and individual goal structures on learning disabled and nondisabled students. Exceptional Children,52,103–114.
49. Cooperative Learning Centre. (1991). Questionnaire on the Use of Cooperative Learning. Minneapolis: Cooperative Learning Centre, University of Minnesota.
50. Du, S. (1998). The effects of cooperative learning on adult English learning achievement, behavior, and satisfaction. Master's thesis: National Chung Cheng University.
51. Deutsch, M. (1962). Cooperation and trust: some theoretical notes. In M. R. Jones (Ed.), Nebraska symposium on motivation (pp. 275-319). Lincoln, NE: University of Nebraska Press.
52. Dansereau, D. F. (1983). Cooperative learning: Impact on acquisition of knowledge and skills (Report No. 341). Abilene, TX: U. S. Army Research Institute for the Behavioral and Social Sciences. (ERIC Document Reproduction Service No. ED 243 088)
53. Fink, L.D. (2004). Beyond small groups: Harnessing the extraordinary power of learning. In Michaelsen L., Knight, A. & Fink L.D. Team-Based Learning: A transformative use of small groups. Sterling, VA: Stylus Publishing.
54. Feldman, K. A. (1989). The association between student ratings of specific instructional dimensions and student achievement: Refining and extending synthesis of data from multi-section validity studies. Research in Higher Education, 33, 317-375.
55. Gillies, R. (2003b). Structuring cooperative group work in classrooms. International Journal of Educational Research, 39, 35-49.
56. Gillies, R. (2006). Teachers' and students' verbal behaviours during cooperative and small-group learning. British Journal of Educational Psychology, 76, 271-287.
57. Gillies, R. (2008). The effects of cooperative learning on junior high school students' behaviours, discourse, and learning during a science-based learning activity. School Psychology International, 29, 328-347.

58. Hagman, J., & Hayes, J. (1986). Cooperative learning: Effects of task, reward, and group size on individual achievement (Tech. Rep. No. 704). Boise, ID: Scientific Coordination Office, U.S. Army Research Institute for the Behavioral and Social Sciences. (ERIC Document Reproduction Service No. ED 278720)

59. Johnson, R. T., & Johnson, D. W. 1986. Action Research: Cooperative Learning in the Science Classroom. Science and Children, 24, 31–32.

60. Johnson, D., Johnson, R. & Holubec, E., 1993. Cooperation in the Classroom. Boston: Allyn & Bacon. Sinhanayok, C., and Hooper, S., 1988. The Effects of Cooperative Learning and Learner Control on Students' Achievement, Options Selections and Attitudes. Educational Technology Research and Development, 46(2), 17–32.

61. Johnson, D. & Johnson, R. (1990). Cooperative learning and achievement. In S. Sharon (Ed.), Cooperative learning: Theory and research (pp. 23-37). New York: Praeger.

62. Johnson, D. W., Johnson, R. T., & Stanne, M. B. (2000). Cooperative learning methods: A meta-analysis. Methods of cooperative learning: What can we prove works? Retrieved August 4, 2000.

63. Kaminski, L.B. (1991). The effect of formal group skill instruction and role development on achievement of high school students taught with cooperative learning. Unpublished doctoral dissertation, Michigan State University.

64. Mercer, N. (1996). The quality of talk in children' collaborative activity in the classroom. Learning and Instruction, 6, 359-377.

65. McPartland, J. M., & Slavin, R. E. (1990). Policy perspectives: Increasing achievement of at-risk students at each grade level. Washington, DC: Information Services, Office of Educational Research and Improvement.

66. Newmann, F.M., & Thompson, J. (1987). Effects of cooperative learning on achievement in secondary schools: A summary of research. Madison, WI: University of Wisconsin, National Center on Effective Secondary Schools.

67. Robinson, A. (1990). Cooperation or exploitation? The argument against cooperative learning for talented students. Journal for the Education of the Gifted, 14(1), 9-27.

68. Rogers, K. B. (1991a). Cooperative versus individualistic learning in English: Which works? Paper presented at the annual meeting of the National Association for Gifted Children, Kansas City, MO.

69. Slavin, Robert E. (1990) Cooperative Learning: Theory, Research, and Practice. Allyn and Bacon, Toronto, ISBN 0-13-172594-7 Salend,

D., & Sonnenschein, P. (1989). Validating the effectiveness of a cooperative learning strategy through direct observation. Journal of School Psychology, 27,47-58.

70. Smith, K., Johnson, D.W., & Johnson, R. (1982). The effects of cooperative and individualistic instruction on the achievement of handicapped, regular, and gifted students. Journal of Social Psychology, 116, 277-283.
71. Stevens, R., Slavin, R., & Farnish, A. (1991). The effects of cooperative learning and directed instruction in reading comprehension strategies on main idea identification. Journal of Educational Psychology, 83, 8-16.
72. Slavin, R. E. (1996). Research on cooperative learning and achievement: What we know, what we need to know. Contemporary Educational Psychology, 21, 43–69.
73. Slavin, R. E., Hurley, E. A., & Chamberlain, A. M. (2003). Cooperative learning and achievement: theory and research. In Handbook of psychology: Educational psychology, Vol. 7 (pp. 177-198). New York, US: John Wiley & Sons.
74. Towns, M. H.; Kreke, K.; Fields, A. J. Chem. Ed. 2000, An Action Research Project: Student Perspectives on Small-Group Learning in Chemistry. 77, 111–115.
75. Tang, C. (1998). Effects of collaborative learning on the quality of assignments. In B. Dart & G. Boulton-Lewis (Eds.), Teaching and Learning in Higher Education (pp. 102–123). Melbourne, Australia: The Australian Council for Education Research Ltd.
76. Tannen, K., Chatman, L., Allen, D. (2003). Approaches to Cell Biology Teaching: Cooperative Learning in the Science Classroom—Beyond Students Working in Groups. Cell Biology Education, 2(1), 1-5.
77. Urdan, T. (1999) (Ed.), Advances in motivation and achievement, Vol. 11: Motivation in context. Stanford, CT: JAI Press.
78. Webb, N. (1992). Testing a theoretical model of student interaction and learning in small groups. In R. Hertz-Lazarowitz, & N. Miller (Eds.), Interaction in cooperative groups (pp. 102e119). Cambridge, UK: Cambridge University Press.
79. Wilson, J., & Wing Jan, L. (2008). Smart thinking: Developing reflection and meta-cognition. Carlton, Victoria, Australia: Curriculum Corporation
80. Yager, S., Johnson, R.T., Johnson, D.W., & Snider, B. (1986). The impact of group processing on achievement in cooperative learning. Journal of Social Psychology, 126, 389-397.

81. Aggarwal J.C., (1955), Essentials of Educational Psychology, Vikas Publishing House Pvt.Ltd., New Delhi.

82. Aggarwal J.O., (1991), Essentials of Educational Psychology, Vikas Publishing House, New Delhi.

83. Best, John W., (1997), Research Methodology, New Jerssy Englewood Clifts.

84. Boudah, (1999), "Learning Strategies" Review of Educational Research.

85. Chang, Chun-Yen, Cheng, Wei-Ying, (2008), Science Achievement and Students' Self-confidence and Interest in Science: A Taiwanese representative sample study. International Journal of Science Education 30 (9), 1183-1200.

86. Chen, Xinyin, (1995), Social functioning and Adjustment in Chinese Children, journal of development Psychology, vol.31, No.4, pp.531-39.

87. Cheng, H., Furnham A., (2002), Personality, peer relations, and self confidence as predictors of happiness and loneliness. Journal of Adolescence, 25 (3), 327-339.

88. Chauhan S.S., (1988), Advanced Educational Psychology, Vikas Publishing House Pvt., Ltd., New Delhi.

89. Chaube S.P., (1992), Experimental Psychology, Lakshmi Narain Agarwall, Agra.

100. Crow and Crow, Adolescent development and adjustment, New York.

101. Dandapani S., (2003), advanced Educational Psychology, Ammol Publication, New Delhi.

102. Ediger, Marlow, (2004), School Climate and Learning Journals of Education Tracks. Vol.3, No.10, P.22, June 2004.

103. Fassett, William E., Olswang, Steven G., (1991), Affiliate Faculty and Student Evaluation, Discipline and Dismissals. American Journal of Research Education, v55 n3 P.11-18.

104. Geeta, Pasteyand Vijayalaxmi, Aminbhavi, (2006), Impact of emotional maturity on stress and self-confidence of adolescents. Journal of the Indian Academy of Applied Psychology.

105. Klever and Phillip, (2009), a study conducted Goal Direction and Effectiveness, Emotional Maturity, and Nuclear Family Functioning. Journal of Material and Family Therapy, v35 n3 p.308-324 Jul 2009.

106. Lee and Sang Kill and Yi, (2011), Family Systems as Predictors of Career Attitude Maturity for Korean High School Students. Asia Pacific Education Review, v11 n2 p.141-150 June 2010

107. Licata, Joseph W., Wildes, James R., (1980), High School Journal, v63 n4 P.146-54.

108. Lieberman, A., Darling-Hammond L., & Zuckerman D., (1991), Early lessons in restructuring schools, New York: National Center for Restructuring Education, Schools, and Teaching, Teachers College, Columbia University.
109. Nelson Laird, Thomas, (2005), College Students' Experiences with Diversity and their Effects on Academic Self-Confidence, Social Agency, and Disposition toward Critical Thinking. Research in Higher Education, 46 (4), 365-387.
110. Raj M., (1996), Encyclopedia Dictionary of Psychology and Education, New Delhi: Anmol publications.
111. Richard, J.K.Ofshe (Ed.) (1973), Interpersonal Behaviour in Small Group, prentice Hall, New York.
112. Shavelson, (2000), 'Self confidence and the interplay of theory and methods' journal of education psychology, V74, P.3-17
113. Tesng, et al., (2011), Social Adjustment among Taiwanese Children with symptoms of ADHD, ODD, and ADHD Co morbid with ODD. Child Psychiatry and Human Development, v42 n2, p.134-151, Apr 2011
114. Wasani et.al., (1991), A text book of Educational Psychology, Mac Millan India Limited, Madras.
115. Wenizel, (1996), Relations of cohension and powers in family dyadas to social emotional adjustment during early adolescence, Journal of research on adolescence. Vol.6, no.2, Pp.225-44.
116. Zimmerman, B.J., (2000), Attaining Self-Regulation: A Social Cognitive Perspective. In M.Boekaerts, P.R.Pintrich, & M.Zeidner, Handbook of Self-Regulation. (Pp.13-35). San Diego, Academic Press.
117. Bailkeri, K. N. (1983): Effect of self- Instructional Remedial Micro Teaching course on the Instructional Competency of in service secondary school mathematics teachers.
118 Bhalwankar, A. G. (1984): A study of Reliability and Validity of the process appraising scale of teacher effectiveness.
119. Balachandran, E. S. (1981): Teaching effectiveness and student evaluation of Teaching, Ph.D., Education, Madras University.
120. Coates, T. I. and Thoresen (1976 spring): Teacher anxiety, A review with recommendation, Review of educational research 49(2), pp.159-184.
121. Cooper, C. Marshal, J. (1976): Occupational sources of stress. A review of the literature relating to coronary heart disease and mental ill health Journal of occupational Psychology, pp.11-28.

122. Cox, T. Mackay, C. J.Cox, S. Watts, C.and Brockley (1978): Stress and wellbeing in schoolteachers psycho-physiological response to occupational stress. Paper presented to the Economic Society Conference, Nottingham University England.

123. Dohrenwend, D. et. al (1981): Stress in the community a report to the president's commission on the accidents at three-mile land. Annual of the New York Academy of Sciences 365, 159-174.

124. Dac, R.C. Passi, B K. and Singh, A. (1982): Effectiveness of different strategies of integration of teaching skills in developing general teaching competency of student's teachers department of teacher education, NCERT.

125. Davis, H. (1964): Evaluation of current practices in evaluating teacher competency, in B. J. Biddle and J. Ellance (Eds). Contemporary research on teacher effectiveness, New York, Holt, Rinehart and Winston.

126. Donald, M. Medley (1982): Teacher Effectiveness" Encyclopedia of Educational Research, Education Harold. E. Mitzel, Vol. 4. Mac millan publishing & Co., New York.

127. Fimian, M. J. and Santoro, T.M. (1983): sources and manifestations of occupational stress and reported by full item special education teachers. Exceptional children, pp. 540-543.

128. Gupta, N. and Beehr, T.A. (1973): "Job stress and employee behavior", Organization behaviors and human performance, pp. 373-387.

129. Girdano, D.E. and Everly, G. S. (1979): Controlling stress and tension, Englewood cliffs, N.J. Prinetice hall.

130. Greenwood, G.E. Olejuik, S. F. and Parkoy, F. W. (1990): Relationship between four teacher efficiency belief patterns and selected teacher characteristics. Journal of research and development in education,23 (2), 102-106.

131. Gupta, S. (1981): A comparative study of Socio-Economic background problems and professional behavior of men women teachers in co-education Institutions at different levels in the state of Haryana, Ph.D., Education, Kurnool University.

132. Gupta, U. (1981): job involvement and need patterns of primary school teachers in relation to teaching effectiveness Ph.D. Education, All Universities.

133. Hodge, J. and Marker (1978): assuring teacher stress; beneficial task for administrator, American secondary Education, 8(4).

134. Joseph schwrzwaldet at stress reaction of school age children to the Bombardment by send missiles journal of Abnormal Psychology 1993, Vol. 102, No.3, 404-410.

135. Kaiser, J.S. and Polezynski, J. J. (1982): Educational stress sources, reaction, preventions. Poe body journal of education 10.
136. Kessler, R. C. Price, R.H. and Wortman, C. B. (1985): social factors in phycho pathology, stress support and coping process, annual review of psychology 36,pp. 531-572.
137. Kryiacane and Suteliffe, J. (1977): Teacher Stress; A review educational review 29.
138. Kryiacau, C. and Sutclifee, J. (1978): Teacher stress; Prevalence, Source and Symptoms, British journal of educational psychology 48.
139. Lazarus,S. Folkman (1984): Stress appraisal and coping, New York Springer publishing company.
140. Lislie Sovoy (1990): "Source of stress on trainee lectures for further and higher education". Journal for Higher education summer (1990).
141. Vene, M.R. (1985): A study of some of the personality components of creative student teacher in relation to their competency towards teaching.
142. Yogendra Kumar and Rattan Lai (1980): Use of micro-teaching in improving general teaching competency of in service teachers.
143. Arnett, J.J. (1999): Adolescent storm and stress, Reconsidered. American Psychologist, pp. 317-326.
144. Folkman, S. and Lazarus, R. S.(1985): If it changes it must be a prosess: Study of emotion and coping during three stages of a college examination. Journal of personality and social psychology, 48, 150-170.
145. Lazarus, R. S. (1993): Coping theory and research: Past, present and future. Psychosomatic Medicine, pp.234-247.

❑❑❑